We Are Pod

injini press

INJINI PRESS

Published by Injini Press
Drink Me Productions Ltd,
10 Blake Court, Wheldrake, York YO19 6BT, United Kingdom

www.moonpooltrilogy.co.uk

First published in Great Britain by Injini Press in 2014
This paperback edition published in 2019

ISBN : 978 0 9552437 5 2

For my family

and for all those who strive to ensure
that our world continues to be home to
leatherback turtles and fin whales,
rhinos and great white sharks,
honey bees and bluefin tuna,
orangutans, dolphins and phytoplankton,
and all the amazing biodiversity
that is threatened and endangered
by human activity today.

Prologue

I carefully drag our keep nets closer to the shore, hook them over the spikes, crawl out of the sea and drop onto the warm shingle beside my laptop,

'No more fish in the sea, no more us, no more you,' Calypso insists.

Here I am in a sheltered cove on an uninhabited island with the turquoise Mediterranean lapping at my feet, chatting with two bottlenose dolphins.

How cool is that? Glad you asked. It's not cool, it's a pain in the butt.

One dolphin is as sociable as a shark with toothache and the other assumes she knows more than I do about everything.

'We can't save all the fish in the Mediterranean. There are only five of us.' I am using sign language, the same as I use with my brother Fred who is deaf.

'Fine. Don't come then,' Steve's retorts, his dorsal fin slicing through the waves, his whistles and clicks picked up by the hydrophone in the water and translated on the laptop in front of me. His head pops up next to Calypso's.

'Do you even know the meaning of the word plan?' I sign.

'Shh, Sam. They're coming,' Calypso shuts us both up. 'I hear the boat.'

'Forget it,' Steve says, slapping his flukes on the water. 'Humans don't care about the sea.'

'Unfair,' I lose my temper. 'You do what you want, all I'm saying is that I am not going on any more mad night-time commando raids on the Mafia's illegal fish pens. It's dangerous and it's pointless. Finished.'

1

Ten metres above our heads the sun has all but set. The last reds and oranges ripple and fade in a criss-crossing geometry of liquid light that skates the surface of a heaving mountain of water.

Calypso and Steve have disappeared ahead. Darkness doesn't bother them, they use echolocation to see in this light. Which is nice.

For them.

Yes I know, I said I wasn't doing this again. It was four against one. I could either stay alone on the boat to wait an hour to see if any of them returned, or I could join them.

Choices, choices.

Rafael pulls my sleeve. I follow his gaze. A huge, steel coloured cylinder hangs in the sea, thirty metres deep and twenty across. The cylinder is revolving at high speed and it's alive. Thirty tonnes or more of bluefin tuna, the fastest muscle in the sea, powering round like motorbikes on the wall of death in a fairground.

Now I see Calypso and Steve. The dolphins are way below, smudges surging like velvet bullets from the depths.

Dad points down. 'Remember, we have only twenty five minutes.' He signs.

We drop until we are level with the bottom of the net. Slashing through the mesh, hand over hand, we cut a wide circle some three metres across. As soon as we have completed our job, Calypso and Steve swim through the hole and disappear into the mass of tuna.

Rafael and I hold open the hole, preventing it from collapsing while Dad secures the net against itself with plastic clips. The fish stream out in a burnished pewter blur, driven by the dolphins. Bluefin tuna can grow over one and a half metres long. Their speed is terrifying, if one misses its line and swims into us it will be like being smacked by a speeding train.

Above us is the faintest outline of the buoys and pipes that hold the top of the net in a circle on the surface. Beneath the buoys are the swirling tuna and an occasional darting dolphin silhouette. The flow of fish thins as the net empties. Dad and Rafael exchange thumbs up signs. The dolphins flash past us, clicking loudly. What will that look like on the flippercams the dolphins are both carrying?

The second net goes as smoothly as the first. How many tuna are we saving from the illegal smuggling operation that is emptying the Mediterranean in order to provide Japan with sushi? Hundreds? Tens of thousands?

Rafael points towards a third net, some twenty metres away.

'Seven minutes,' I sign, checking my dive computer. 'You promised.'

'One more net,' Dad signs.

Like now is all that matters. Like tomorrow's Big Event doesn't exist. I swear, if I could throw a punch underwater, I would.

Calypso returns towards us and Dad signs to her. I notice the way she positions herself in the water, left flipper down, head at an angle, as she emits a stream of clicks.

'Understood,' Dad signs back.

We follow the dolphins towards the third spinning column, barely visible now in the enveloping indigo gloom. This is like drowning in ink. Pretty soon we won't even know which way is up, except by following the direction of our bubbles. Or something else's bubbles.

Steve passes close by, the pressure of his movement through the water pushing me back into the net before I see it. Dad grabs my shoulders and looks into my face. 'OK?' he signs.

I nod. 'I lost my balance. I'm OK.'

'The last net. I promise.'

Our serrated blades rip the mesh of the net. I glance at Rafael. Focused, face taut, body tense. Beneath him his flipper tips warp back and forth.

The net falls open. Once again the dolphins brush past us into the mass of swirling tuna. Secure the hole and we've finished, I tell myself, grabbing the clips from my belt and passing them through the mesh and tying back. The net jerks violently in my hands and the clip I am holding falls from my grasp, disappearing into the gloom beneath me.

Another spasm of the mesh.

I look up. Everything is shades of blue but I can make out a dolphin silhouette thrashing back and forth above me. One of the dolphins is caught in the net. Without thinking, I dive through the hole and swim upwards, somehow avoiding the steady stream of tuna coming in the opposite direction. Five metres up I reach Calypso. A metal rod half a metre long has passed through her flukes and pinned her to the mesh. Seeing me approach she fires off a torrent of whistles and clicks. I cannot understand her.

'It's an arrow,' I explain. (What is the sign for harpoon?) 'The tip is serrated so I cannot pull it out. I am going to push it through.'

Has she understood? She waits patiently as I force the harpoon down through her flukes. All is going well until it jams; the last two centimetres of the harpoon are fatter than the shaft.

Beneath us Dad and Rafael are holding the net open as the escaping tuna flow out. Above us a wedge-shaped shadow moves on the surface. A boat.

Grabbing the harpoon from below I yank at it to pull it through. It won't budge. I have no choice. I pull my dive knife from its sheath and, muttering a silent apology, I plunge the tip of the blade into Calypso's flukes, next to the embedded harpoon. She flinches. A cloud of blood forms in the water. I sheathe the knife. The cut has made the difference. This time the end of the harpoon passes through and Calypso's flukes are free. As she swims away towards the hole, a blur of movement catches my eye. Another harpoon? I head down towards the others.

Coming out into the open sea, I see Dad has a harpoon buried in his leg. Shocked, I stop too close to the hole in the net. A third harpoon spears a huge tuna coming out behind me, throwing it off balance. Another dark cloud blossoms. A large cold eye fixes on me momentarily. The thrashing tail smacks against my chest then the tuna has gone, tumbling into the darkness below.

'Go Sam. Go now,' Dad is signing.

Concussed, I turn to Rafael, who grabs me and pulls me back. Away from the net. Away from Dad. Suddenly a column light beams down from above us. A searchlight? A flare? Within the net the remaining trapped fish are a frenzy in silhouette. Like an exploding nail bomb.

'Where is Steve?' I sign.

'Leave, Sam. Now,' Dad orders. 'I follow you.'

No, I've lost you once before. Not again.

Rafael pulls me back and points to his watch.

He is right, with all the extra energy I have expended my tanks must be almost empty. We leave. The adrenalin is really pumping. We are swimming fast. We can no longer see the net, but we can still see the glow of the lights shining down. I check my underwater compass, heading west. I want to go up, to escape this liquid prison and breathe fresh air. Rafael holds me down.

It's my Dad back there, dying with a harpoon in his leg I sign furiously. Rafael doesn't understand sign language. I push him in the chest and swim away. Almost immediately my arms and legs snarl up in something I cannot see. I flail about like a fly in a web.

Desperate but dumb, says the little voice in my head. But little voices are there to be ignored, aren't they?

In seconds I am completely snared and unable to move. I close my eyes. When I open them again I am looking straight at Rafael's facemask.

He removes the regulator from his mouth. 'Den,' he seems to say.

My face betrays total incomprehension. After taking a breath of oxygen from his regulator Rafael tries again. *Led* or *Leg*? I still don't get it.

He ducks out of view and reappears holding something up to my face. Got it! Net. He's saying *net*. I nod and relax my body while Rafael hacks at the mesh. A dark silhouette glides overhead. We are being hunted. Please don't let them switch on their searchlight. Where are the others?

One arm comes free. I grab Rafael's wrist. He pulls his hand away to continue cutting. In the distance, back the way we have come there is a flash of light. A few moments later we feel a shock wave buffet us.

An explosion? Where's Dad?

I am free of the net. We move up to a couple of meters below the waves and keep swimming away from the nets. You use less oxygen closer to the surface.

One second I'm breathing, the next there is nothing left in my tanks. Head spinning, I power upwards. My head breaks the surface. I rip out my regulator and gasp huge lungfuls of air. Rafael appears beside me.

'Look, there is the rock. Over there,' he says, pointing.

We have swum too far south. The headland is maybe a hundred metres to our right. Behind it I can make out the prow of our boat.

We swim in silence. Looking back we catch glimpses of three large boats, appearing then disappearing in the swell some three hundred meters away.

Reaching our boat, La Vita Nuova, we are both too tired to haul ourselves up out of the water. We cling to her anchor rope, catching our breath.

'Hey,' shouts a voice above us.

The silhouetted figure of a diver is pointing a gun at my face.

2

Vicki Gutner makes a show of tidying her desk. Not that there is anything to tidy. No photos of loved ones; there are no loved ones, unless you include an extravagantly expensive Scappa mountain bike, with its bespoke made-to-measure carbon fibre frame, or her lime green Porsche 911, or the Aster Cucine kitchen with its lacquered walnut cabinets. Gutner loves things not people. Photos of things are not what you put on your office desk, and her things are nobody else's business. No pens or paper to stash away other than the dossier she has just printed, which she slides into her briefcase. She writes everything on the tablet she carries with her at all times; Gutner has learned the hard way never to put waste paper in a litterbin.

The organisation's motto is Trust no-one. New recruits take this to refer to 3-TEC's many enemies: terrorists, nosy governments, old clients, peaceniks, international courts, and so on. The motto does refer to them but, most of all, it is a reminder that even within the organisation you are on your own.

She drops her lukewarm black coffee and the plastic sushi box in the bin. As she reaches the door she checks her watch. Ten minutes early.

Standing in the descending lift, clutching her briefcase, Gutner reflects on the dullness of the building. An air-conditioned void that smells of nothing and belongs nowhere. Her blurred reflection in the lift wall sums everything up perfectly, a soft-focused shadowy and anonymous functionary dressed in blue, entombed in a grey polished metalled surface.

Gutner steps out into basement level 5 and takes a seat facing the twin doors. The receptionist glances up then returns to filing her purple nails.

'They are ready for you now,' she says on hearing the buzzer.

Gutner pushes the double doors and crosses the threshold.

Ten of the other eleven chairs are occupied by the intelligence committee which includes three other members of her department: Watson, Kovacs, and Messi. Gutner sits down and pulls the report from her briefcase.

The table and all the chairs are made from transparent plastic. No hidden surfaces to conceal bugs or listening devices. No other furniture. The sound of waves washing a beach emanates from speakers buried in the walls, producing a blanket of white noise that cloaks any conversation and renders any covert listening or recording device, whether hidden about someone's person or in a briefcase, useless. Conversations in this room stay in this room.

In the twelfth chair, at the far end of the table, sits the Head of Operations, Major Tenebris. A night photograph of the organisation's headquarters projected onto the wall behind his chair leaves him in silhouette except for the top of his bald head which glows the same colour as the screen. A thin laser light set in the ceiling points down at his notes. The light reflecting back from the paper lights his face from below, lending his face a ghoul-like appearance.

Aside from the second focussed beam of laser light that hits the surface of the table just in front of her, and into which Gutner pushes her report, the rest of the room is lit only by the giant screen, leaving all of the faces around the table largely in shadow.

'The short version, thank you,' says the figure at the other end of the table.

'Yes, Sir.' Gutner glances at her notes. 'It is now twelve days since the Dauntless was sunk in a harbour on the island of Lipari, with the loss of thirteen lives. These included Major Richards, Ruth Winters, and the vessel's crew and technicians. The incident happened roughly ten hours after the capture of Michel Blanchard, his daughter Sam, and one of the assets stolen by Blanchard several weeks previously. The explosion on the Dauntless originated in the chamber housing the moon pool where, it is believed, Blanchard and daughter were being interrogated and where the asset was situated. Forensic examination has confirmed the deaths of Richards and Winters ...'

'Their bodies have been identified?'

'Small fragments of flesh were found on the sea bed and …'

'Understood, thank you.'

'We believe Richards and Winters were killed by sharks rather than ...'

'Carry on.'

'The rest of the crew died in the explosion.'

'Blanchard, the daughter, and the dolphins?'

'One dolphin, Sir. They only captured …'

'Were their remains identified?'

'No, Sir. The explosion itself and the sea compromised the scene. Several crew members have not been formally identified either. '

'So you abandoned the search?'

'No, Sir. I checked the listings of all passengers on the ferries leaving the island of Lipari and …'

'What if they didn't leave by ferry?' Tenebris cuts her off.

'I raised the same issue,' Gutner counters.

She glances at Major Watson. What she can see of his thin-lipped smile resembles a ragged tear in a sheet of paper; he has been itching to see her fail from the moment she arrived in Sicily. Beside him is Paolo Messi, a jowly-faced specialist in disinformation, who sports a thin moustache like a caterpillar on his upper lip. They have set her up. Messi's face is expressionless. Cowards. Apparently Watson isn't intelligent enough to realise that, as her line manager, any failure on her part will also be his.

'The island has no viable airport,' Gutner continues. 'All visitors and the locals travel by sea. Since Blanchard and his daughter, if they survived the explosion, were fugitives with no transport of their own they would have …'

'Stolen a boat perhaps?'

'There were no thefts reported,' she says. 'All boats sold or hired have been accounted for.'

'How many other boats went down in the explosion that night?'

'Three. All small fishing vessels moored close to the Dauntless. The owners reported the losses.'

'And you investigated?'

'Debris floating in the harbour. Satellite imagery before and after the explosion. Both confirmed that three boats were missing.'

'On the seabed.'

'Sir?'

'You checked the seabed?'

He senses her hesitation. Behind him, the screen changes to show an ugly harbour, an abandoned pumice mine scarring the hill behind an old factory, its glassless windows staring blindly out to sea like the empty sockets in a skull. A long rusting jetty juts out into the grey winter sea like a broken tibia, offering partial shelter to a cluster of cowering fishing boats.

'You identified the wreckage of four vessels on the seabed here at Porticello; the Dauntless and three other boats? You didn't assume that the owners were telling the truth. Insurance claims by opportunistic fishermen don't slip past you, do they?'

As Tenebris moves his head to glance at the screen, Gutner catches sight of the long scar that runs down the left hand side of his face from the top of his head to the corner of his mouth.

'The satellite imagery clearly showed that three boats, plus the Dauntless, were missing the morning after the explosion,' she says. 'As I explained the evidence was compromised by …'

Tenebris lifts his hand to silence her. 'Within the next twelve hours I want to know which of those other boats moored near her did not sink. I want photographs, owners' names, length, draft and beam, paint colour. Everything, including how many forks there are in the cutlery drawer in the galley. Do I make myself clear?'

Across the table Watson parades his thin smile.

'Yes, Sir,' Gutner replies.

'And when we have that information, I want the missing vessel found and destroyed, along with its occupants.'

The screen behind Tenebris changes again, to show close up photos of Michel Blanchard and his daughter, Sam, on board the Dauntless. Gutner stands and opens her briefcase.

'Before you go.' Tenebris turns to the others in the room. 'These dolphins carry implanted GPS tracking devices, do they not?'

Glances are exchanged between several members of the committee.

'So why haven't we found them?' Tenebris shouts at the top of his voice.

Several faces flinch involuntarily.

'It is my understanding,' Gutner says, 'that both tracking devices are currently situated off the coast of Libya and have not moved for seven weeks. We must conclude that either both animals have died and that the dolphin captured two weeks ago was a different animal, or we must assume that the implants have been physically removed and abandoned on the seabed.'

'Why wasn't I told about this?'

Gutner doesn't answer. She doesn't have to. She pushes the report back into her briefcase and stares at Watson, who is pulling uncomfortably at the collar of his shirt, the smile having vanished from his lips. Through the transparent table she sees his knees fidgeting up and down.

3

'No, that's it. You carry on playing Journey to the Bottom of the Sea, that's great,' I shout across the cabin.

'Try counting to ten.'

'Look at us, Dad. You're sitting there with a harpoon in your leg and I could have been killed three times in the past two weeks, as could that idiot at the wheel. Ten minutes ago you were pointing a gun at my head.'

'Basic precautions.'

'This isn't a war zone. Look at my lips, fifteen, too young to die.'

'No-one is too young too die.'

'Oh, great.'

'You're upset.' Rafael cuts in.

'Wow, you're wasted on a small boat. You should have your own television series. Rafael Santoni, tabloid talk show host exposes marine madness.' I turn to Dad. 'And you're no better than he is.'

Rafael and Dad are both speechless, which suits me. I storm out of the cabin, slamming the door. Finding space out on deck isn't easy, there is stuff everywhere, ropes, nets, and provisions. The more rubbish we have on deck, the more space we have below. That is the theory.

I find a crate, turn it over and sit down. We are knee deep in fish crates, living from selling mullet and sea bream in small towns as we make our way up the Italian coast. Steve and Calypso make up for what we lack in fishing skills. As long as we cast the nets, the dolphins locate the fish and drive them to us.

We are heading northwest back to the cove, the moon at our backs, and the island between us and the mafia's fish pens. The sound of the engine and the wash of the sea against the bows of the boat have a hypnotic effect and eventually I calm down enough to notice the Milky Way overhead, sprayed across the night sky like graffiti.

I stand up and look towards the cabin window. Lit by the single overhead bulb, Rafael is smiling as Dad, with his back to me, makes expansive gestures with his hands. Boys' toys technology talk or some sad comments about the girl who can't take the pressure.

Rafael. What can I say? Think Italian version of Shaggy out of Scooby Doo. Add skinny nerd, English international school, blond fringe, gadget geek, and emotional pygmy, and you have him nailed. Oh, and if they sold rubber ties he would wear one with his dry suit when we are diving.

A burst of clicks. I look down and see Calypso riding the bow waves. Without the translator software I understand only the most basic sounds, our names, *yes*, *no*, and the words for '*fish anyone*?'

'Sam … Sam … Michel.'

'He's fine,' I sign. "Where's Steve?' But Calypso has already gone.

The sea is jet black except for the glow in the boat's wash, a magical bioluminescent trail created by plankton churned up by our passing. We are fast approaching the safety of the cove. The pitch of the engine drops as our speed slows to negotiate the rocks. Then suddenly we are picking up speed again and passing by. A hand on my shoulder makes me jump.

'We've removed the harpoon,' Rafael says.

'Why aren't we stopping?'

'Change of plan. Your dad wants to put space between us and the mafia. You know, a centimetre to the left and that harpoon was hitting an artery.'

Too much information.

'And he says don't worry about tomorrow,' Rafael smiles.

So now Dad is talking family stuff with Rafael. Tomorrow is the big day I have been dreaming of since I was six years old. Dad has begged me to stop going on about it, but he is discussing it with Rafael. Great.

'Tell me,' I say, using a fingernail to prise a flake of paint off the gunwale, 'if the man who worked out how to communicate with another species and the world's first talking dolphins died together in a fishing net trying to save a bunch of glass-eyed tuna, how many points out of ten would you give them?'

Rafael doesn't like confrontation, particularly when it is between my Dad and me. 'Steve is missing,' he says, ignoring me. 'He pulled your dad to safety then vanished. I haven't even removed his flippercam. Did you know that dolphins swim three times faster than humans?'

Two can play change the subject. 'For Dad and the dolphins, everything is a combat mission. Here's a target, let's attack. It's all they know. They're on self-destruct and can't see the big picture. Somehow we have to reach out and get on the news, Rafael. Win people over. Could we post the flippercam footage of the tuna raid on social networks? I mean how long have people talked about meeting other intelligent life in the universe? It's right here. If people knew that, they would protect us.'

'The optimism of the innocent.'

Dad is leaning against the cabin doorway, his leg heavily strapped.

'She's got a point,' Rafael says. 'People do love dolphins.'

'People eat dolphins,' Dad retorts. 'We send them on combat missions in war zones, we make them jump through hoops, and we catch them in our nets. We suffocate them with pollution, destroy their fishing grounds, and flood the seas with noise from ships and underwater sonar and drilling.'

'The public doesn't do that.'

'What were you both expecting? Open arms? An interview on Newsbeat? Grow up. Everyone loves tigers, but in ten years they'll all be gone.'

'How about an e-petition?' I suggest. 'In those wildlife films they …'

Dad laughs dismissively. 'That's the problem. We see these animals in films, photos, computer games, zoos, and museums. We read about them in books and poems. We name sports teams after them, you kids use them as screensavers. They're everywhere. They fill our imaginations and our nightmares. Who needs the real thing anymore? Same goes for rhinos, elephants, and everything else that ever walked or flew or swam. Including dolphins. Welcome to virtuality.'

'Do you even know what an e-petition is?' I challenge Dad.

There is a wild glow in his eyes, he was drinking something strong while guiding Rafael through the process of removing the harpoon from his leg.

'Sam was saying that …' Rafael starts.

'Don't waste your time, he's not listening.' I cut in.

Long after the other two have gone back inside, I am still out on deck, mulling stuff over. I am as pleased as they are to free all those tuna and I know that Dad is well aware of the value of what he and Calypso and Steve have achieved in inter-species communication. The trouble is that Dad has become too cynical and tired to believe that anyone else will care, and he has convinced himself that his enemies won't stop until we are all dead. On that, unless we change our game plan, he is probably right.

4

Hours later, as dawn breaks, I am back out on deck, thinking deep thoughts. The sea does that to people. It's the big sky, and the horizon spreading in all directions, and all the possible journeys that lie ahead, that does it. I am thinking about how we have changed the name of the boat to La Vita Nuova, which means new life in Italian, when Dad appears.

'Peace offering?' He is holding two steaming mugs. I take one. Hot chocolate. Dad sits down beside me and tries to get his leg comfortable. 'Before you ask, I haven't forgotten about today. And, before I forget, what you did to rescue Calypso yesterday was amazing. I'm proud of you. Rafael's ready for us. Can you help me up?'

A few kilometres to our right a hump of land appears and disappears as the boat rides the swell. The air is suddenly full of loud death metal guitars.

'That's Elba. We'll change course soon.' Dad says, looking towards the cabin and pulling a face.

Inside Rafael is busy doing what he does best, making gadgets work. The table is covered with various bits of kit.

Dad points at the radio. Rafael turns the music down. Dad shakes his head and makes a rotating gesture with his right hand. Sighing, Rafael turns the music off altogether.

'This is a game changing scenario.' Rafael says, squeezing a small iPad into what looks like a hot water bottle with a window. 'You'll see, old man.'

'If you say so.'

'I do. How long were you a prisoner?'

'Nine years.' Dad taps a syncopated rhythm out on the edge of the table with his fingertips. 'Bossa nova. That's real music. Sophisticated, sexy, and clever.'

'Nine years! Wow, you've missed so much. Sam, pass me that.'

'Like bone soup?' I ask, handing Rafael the receiver, which is not much bigger than a matchbox.

'Bossa nova not osso buco,' Rafael retorts. 'And it's not a soup, it's a sauce.' He connects the receiver to the tablet, switches everything on, seals the waterproof housing and tightens the straps. 'These tie the tablet to the scuba tanks. The batteries should be good for three hours. Where's the hydrophone?' Rafael picks up a tube the size of a small torch and secures it to the side of the iPad housing. 'Look, it's a third of the size of yours, Michel. And this one is wireless.'

'OK, but mine is carved from a single slab of fossilised lava; more durable and … and you can use it as a life raft in an emergency.'

They exchange smiles as boxers do to psych each other out before a fight.

'Sam, can you bring me some water?'

I step outside, fill a bucket with seawater, come back inside and place it on the table in front of Rafael.

'Ready?' He gives us a thumbs up. I nod, and he drops the tablet in the bucket.

'No, not like that,' Dad says, fishing the tablet out of the bucket and hobbling outside before either of us can stop him. We are coming through the doorway as Dad hurls the tablet into the sea, falling over in the process.

'What did you do that for?' I shout, watching the kit slowly sinking beneath the surface.

Dad shrugs then reaches for the gunwale to pull himself up.

I look about wildly for a pole. There is nothing long enough and by the time I turn back the iPad has disappeared from view.

'Remind me. It's watertight to what depth?' Dad asks.

'Fifty metres,' Rafael answers, his voice flat.

'Are you expecting someone to dive in?' I ask.

Dad smiles and rubs his head.

'You are insane,' I scream, lunging at him.

At that moment the water by the boat bursts upwards, soaking me to the skin as Calypso appears, balancing the iPad on her snout. In one deft movement she twists and tosses the tablet and its connected hydrophone towards Dad who catches it and hands it to me. On the screen are the words, 'Why didn't you tell me you were going to drop this? I nearly missed it.'

'So?' Rafael's grin is wider than a coat hanger.

'OK, it's dry,' Dad says, inspecting the tablet. 'You win. Well done.'

Rafael turns to me. 'Now we will all know exactly what the dolphins are saying when we are underwater. Three sets of wireless underwater earphones, so we won't even need to look at the screen. The computer will translate and beam the audio straight to our ears.'

'The Nobel Prize for total geniosity is yours.' I hand Rafael the tablet. 'Now can we have breakfast?'

'I still want you both to work learning to understand their language directly for yourselves.'

'Yes, Dad, but that is going to take years. In the meantime …'

'… technology liberation scenario.'

'What he says,' I agree. 'And since you are the tech guru, Rafael, can you switch my Dad back to his default factory settings? His random access memory chip is fried; hurling iPads into the sea is seriously fruity.'

'Fruity?' Rafael says, like he has never heard the expression before. He glances down at the tablet in his hand. 'New message,' he says, passing the tablet to me.

The text reads, 'Michel, we need to talk. Something has happened.' I pass the tablet to Dad.

'OK. Give me a few minutes.' Dad signs to Calypso. He turns to me. 'I need to eat.'

I scramble some eggs while Dad corrects our heading and Rafael dismantles the kit. To tell the truth, I am not sure I will ever learn to recognise many words in the noises the dolphins make. Even slowed down and dropped in pitch, the noises they make sound nothing like human language. For a start, there are no consonants or vowels because they don't make noises with their mouths and they have no lips. Dad has five years head start on us, and he still finds it difficult.

'Is it true that dolphins can eavesdrop each other's echolocation?' Rafael says with his mouth full.

'One dolphin can send out a burst of sonar and then draw another dolphin's attention to the echo bouncing back,' Dad replies. 'The second dolphin knows not only where an object is but also its shape, size, density and texture. So yes.'

'Has the military tried building a device that can mimic that? So we could listen in as well?'

'Funny you should ask. When I first …'

I am no longer listening, more interested in the meeting planned for lunchtime than I am in sonar use among cetaceans. I leave them to it and go back outside. Minutes later the cabin door opens.

'Breathe deeply the beauty of the Earth, Sam. We're here to protect her,' Dad says, behind me.

'Total hippie,' I turn and smile.

'Guilty as charged.' He smiles back. 'You know, you were right last night about needing a plan and there is one. Remember Carla Biseti?'

'It's hard to forget someone who introduces herself by pushing you over, then shoves an envelope from your long dead father into your hand.'

'She promised that if I could get out of Italy alive with the dolphins she would make sure we were safe.'

'So apart from the fact that she was shot dead three weeks ago we are home and dry. Who did she say would help?'

'To protect them and to protect you that information stays in here.' Dad taps the side of his head. A cloud passes across his face. 'We are not out of danger yet.'

'How does today …'

'Don't worry bout today, Sam, just let it happen. It will be fine. You remember the moon pool, when you were small?"

It has given me nightmares for years. We were in Scotland, making sandcastles on vast beaches, cowering from the biting wind behind a stripy canvas screen, me driving Mum nuts by playing a set of bagpipes made from a carrier bag and some drinking straws. My sixth birthday.

Dad had taken me aboard the research ship he worked on. The week he disappeared. We tossed fish at the dolphins gathered alongside the boat then went below deck through doors with wheels set in the middle of them until, at the bottom of the ship, we reached a darkened room containing a secret pool that opened directly into the sea. A moon pool.

'That's how they kidnapped me. Three of them came up out of the moon pool, shackled me, forced me into scuba gear and threw me in the water. They had a small submarine a few hundred metres away. The next time I set foot on dry land I was in the Middle East.'

Why tell me all this now?

'You could have shouted for help,' I tell him.

'They wanted marine biologists to train dolphins for use in the Iraq war.'

‘You should have refused.’

Dad’s face is drawn. ‘The daytime temperature in Oman is frightening. Do you know how long a human survives fifty degrees in a desert?’

‘So you gave up and strapped bombs to them and did all those other things that mark humans out as the most intelligent beings on the planet.’

Dad sighs. ‘I taught Calypso and Steve sign language because it meant we could communicate underwater without drawing the attention of the guards. Once they understood the limits of human hearing they adjusted the pitch of their vocalisations. We worked for hours, months, years, teaching each other, without anyone else having any idea what we were doing. Developing the translation software that we’re using on the laptops took three years. I never gave up, Sam. And neither did they.’

A burst of clicks behind me signals that we are not alone. ‘Give me a couple of minutes,’ Dad signs over my shoulder.

I turn in time to see the two dolphins disappear below the waves.

‘Why Calypso and Steve?’ I ask. ‘Why did you call him Steve?’

‘I knew a Steve at school. Same easy going magnetic personality, charming, always keen to help, optimistic and …’

‘Yeah, OK. I get it.’

The cabin door bangs open.

‘You two need to come in. You won’t believe this,’ Rafael says.

5

Gutner stands to attention and focuses on keeping her eyes open. She has spent the night in a helicopter, island hopping with a team of balaclava wearing commandos, banging on doors and dragging people out of bed. Tracking down all the individual fishermen who own boats moored by the old pumice mine on the north east coast of Lipari has been far from easy, not least because many of the registrations are fakes. The mafia's stranglehold is everywhere; many islanders don't even sneeze without permission. She and her team have been forced to be at their most persuasive. There are a number of people waking up this morning with black eyes, aching ribs and, in one unfortunate instance, broken fingers. It is 10am; she hasn't slept in nearly thirty hours.

'You are sure that this is the one?' Tenebris asks.

'Sorry?' Gutner answers with jolt, realising that she has slipped out of consciousness momentarily.

'This is the right boat?'

'Yes, Sir. Last seen three days ago. In Anzio. They were selling fish in the harbour. A man and two teenagers, one male, one female. The Blanchards collected Rafael Santoni and took him with them as they made their escape.'

On the desk in front of Tenebris a red light is flashing on one of the telephones. Behind him, mounted on the grey concrete wall is a large photograph of a giant spider crab taken on the seabed somewhere, bright vermillion against an inky black sea.

Finishing the first page of her report, Tenebris reaches out and lifts the receiver. He listens a few seconds then mutters 'just do it', replaces the receiver in its cradle and finishes reading.

'What do you suppose to be an appropriate punishment for this failure?' His voice is calm and measured.

Gutner stares ahead; rhetorical questions don't require an answer. She notices that he is wearing a sharkskin suit. She has a pencil skirt in the same silk and wool mix; an appropriate material for them both.

'Anzio is five hundred kilometres north. They could be in France by now. Who told you to let them go?'

He wants a scapegoat. But will he protect her? She has seen too many unfortunate accidents where witnesses have disappeared, fallen off cliffs or under buses.

'I volunteer to find the Blanchards, Sir. Wherever they are, give me the job.'

'You want me to reward failure with responsibility?'

Tenebris crosses the room and disappears behind her. Gutner fights the urge to turn, to face him; she knows better.

'Six.' She stares straight ahead at the empty desk. 'You said you wanted to know how many forks there were in the cutlery drawer. There were six. I know all there is to know about the boat, the Pagano family that own it, their dog, Vedette, and their little business smuggling watches and designer clothes. The boat is called Stella di Natale.'

'If no-one has changed the name.'

'I know the dolphins are a significant asset,' Gutner continues, 'trained to locate and plant mines and to protect our clients' vessels from undersea attack. They must not fall into enemy hands. I have studied the files we have on Blanchard's activities in Libya and the Persian Gulf. I have …'

'Your colleagues,' a gravel whisper in her left ear stops her in mid-flow, 'threw you to the lions. I don't need another spineless runner, Gutner. I want an assassin. We have already lost too much time. You will take Watson and Messi with you and …'

'No,' she dares to cut him off. 'With respect, Sir, the boat is not travelling very quickly; the targets are being very cautious. Catching both humans and dolphins requires patience and skill, not a mass assault. I want to work alone.'

Tenebris is still behind her. His breath caresses her neck, like a panther smelling its prey. She clenches her jaw and stays silent. She feels him withdraw but instead of relaxing she becomes tenser.

'I don't want them caught, I want them killed. You will wear an electronic tracker, which security will implant for you. We wouldn't want to lose you.'

'Lose me, Sir?'

'You have twenty six hours, till midday tomorrow.' He steps out from behind her and shows her the door. 'After that I will send Watson and Messi to collect you. You can assume that your safety will not be uppermost on their list of priorities.'

If Watson and Messi are sent after her, they should assume that their safety will not be high on her list of priorities either, Gutner thinks to herself.

6

'Is it real?'

'Shh, Sam. I need to think.' Dad adjusts our course then joins us at the galley table, rubbing his eyes. He suddenly looks very tired, like when we found him on the island. 'What's that noise?'

'Stigma. They're an Italian death metal band. They're great, aren't they?'

Dad's look is enough. Rafael turns the radio down then, seeing Dad's face still looks like someone has slapped it, he turns it off.

'Have you asked Calypso? She must have seen it,' I suggest, looking at the image on the laptop screen.

'No. Look at the angle. The flipper cam has twisted underneath her.' Rafael points at the screen. 'The camera is upside down. It's filming behind her.'

'There.' Dad freezes the image. He clicks backwards one frame at a time then plays the film forwards in slo-mo.

Underwater in the open sea there is nothing to give any real sense of scale. It appears fifty centimetres long, maybe longer.

'What is it?' I ask.

'A mechanical fish,' Rafael says. "The CIA and others have been developing them for spying and surveillance. I read about it. There is also a robot jellyfish that can …'

'Forget what it is.' Dad interjects. 'The question is who owns it? And what did they see?'

'It can see?' I ask.

'What would be the point, if it couldn't see?' Rafael says.

The fish is swimming alongside Calypso. It has dropped down into shot from above. Like everything else in the image, it is upside down.

'Maybe it's a trick of the light. Maybe it's just another tuna.'

'No, Sam.' Dad shakes his head.

As if to confirm his words, the fish surges forwards until its eye is almost touching Calypso's flippercam. The iris opens like a camera lens. A dim red light glows within. Infrared night vision. A machine.

In the next frame of video Calypso is again speeding away, and the metal fish is swallowed in the gloom. Dad fast-forwards the film. A flash of light briefly reveals its silhouette some twenty metres behind. A loud audio thump shakes the laptop's speakers. The images continue in silence.

'Why would they be so stupid? A bomb destroys the tuna.'

'It was a small concussion grenade. Anything bigger than that and we would be dead.' Dad crosses the cabin and adjusts our course.

Through the window are two other fishing boats on the same heading as us. My heart skips a beat, I am seeing enemies everywhere.

'Where are Calypso and Steve?' Dad says over his shoulder.

We go out on deck. Calypso appears off the starboard bow.

'Michel, it's important,' Calypso says.

'It has to wait until this afternoon.'

Suddenly there is a huge splash, as Steve leaps out of the water and comes down smashing his flukes hard on the waves. No sign of a flippercam, it must have fallen off.

'Great, a dolphin with anger management issues,' Dad says to me. 'Today is your day from now on.'

'Thanks Dad.'

7

'No, it's up on the right. Rafael and I checked everything yesterday morning.'

I am starting to think Dad would have preferred a son to a daughter. As we reach a junction, the sound of a police siren ricochets off the shop fronts. Unable to tell in which direction the sound is coming from, we stop. Across the street a woman shepherds children into the grocer's shop. The little boy grabs a peach from a box as he disappears inside.

The police car appears from our left and continues on its way, the pitch of the siren dropping as it passes. In the car's wake are two paramedics on mopeds; like pilot fish following a shark. The woman and children emerge from the shop, the boy clutching a huge bar of chocolate.

'Hang on a second. Dad, have you got ten euros?'

I cross the street and run inside. The shop is barely wider than a corridor. The chocolate is close to the till. I spend every last cent of the ten euros, my mouth watering as my haul goes into a large thick brown paper bag.

'OK, we can go.' I pull Dad away from the postcards.

Glancing back down the street I see the harbour and the red prow of La Vita Nuova. With luck, Rafael is making a fortune selling our small catch of mullet, bream and sea bass. Gulls are shrieking above the rooftops. The air smells of pizza, distracting when you are stuffing chocolate in your face.

'Come on, we're late, you know how upset she gets.'

Half an hour from port, Dad decided to shave. I did a double take when he stepped into the galley, hidden away under that grey beard was the father I remembered, and when he smiled I hugged him and began to believe dreams could come true. Here we are now, him limping in the new blue shirt he bought in the market yesterday, me striding in the green dress he bought at the same time and hid away to surprise me with.

The road turns sharply right.

Dad holds me back with his hand. 'New plan.' He swings me round and pulls me into a narrow alley that leads up the hill.

‘Why?’

‘Roadblock.’

‘What roadblock? Who are they?’

‘It doesn’t matter.’

‘If it doesn’t matter then we can walk past.’

‘They’re in uniform, don’t be stupid.’

‘It’s too dangerous.’

‘Sam, if you want to return to the boat and wait there …’

We climb the alley, passing pots of geraniums clinging to window ledges, pushing through tablecloths hanging from washing lines, and emerge onto a street running parallel to the one below.

‘No reason to think that they are looking for us,’ Dad says, unconvincingly.

We reach the Hotel Montefiore, a large imposing building situated in its own grounds, its walls a bright mustard yellow. Two sets of steps with wrought iron railings lead up towards a pair of ornamental orange trees standing sentry at either side of the front door. We step out of the sun and onto a pale cream marble floor. Behind the reception desk stands a man as fat as a hamster, his jowls shaking as he turns towards us.

‘Signor Blanchard, hello again.’

‘Salve. Have they arrived?’

‘An hour ago. Please to go to the terrace.’ The hamster man’s voice is charged with conspiratorial excitement as he ushers us through. ‘Everything is ready. Some drinks perhaps?’ He stops on the threshold and sweeps his hand towards the terrace.

‘Thank you. Champagne, and orange juice for the children. But give us a few moments please.’

‘Such a beautiful day,’ the hamster-faced maître d’ calls out behind us.

There are maybe ten tables in the dappled sunlight beneath the orange trees, four of them occupied; a large family, a young couple, a small dark-haired man in a loud shirt sitting with a red-haired older woman who I decide must be his mother. Water trickles prettily in a stone fountain.

She sits alone beyond the fountain, with her back to us, in her favourite turquoise dress, looking out over the town towards the sea. Her bare arms are pale, Yorkshire suddenly popping up in Italy in mid-winter. On the table beside her is a small espresso with a biscuit balancing precariously on the saucer lip. Somewhere someone is singing opera along to a radio, the voices drifting across the rooftops.

Beside me Dad takes a deep breath, like the first breath you take when you come up out of the sea. When he swallows, his Adam's apple moves, it has been hidden in his beard until now. I squeeze his hand and we step outside, our feet crunching in the gravel. Two metres away we stop.

'Lara.'

She has her hand pressed to her forehead to shield her eyes.

Dad clears his throat. 'Lara,' he says a second time.

'Mum.'

8

She turns slowly. Her eyes glance at Dad then linger on me. She smiles, with her mouth but not with her eyes. I remember that expression from my last day at primary school; all of us in Year Six had sung a song about moving on to our new school and how we were going to be brave and how our whole lives were ahead of us. Mum was in the second row, wearing Dad's absence like a missing limb. When we finished singing I saw that all the parents had the same sad eyes and happy smiles, except for Kate White's mum who was pretending to blow her nose.

'Sam,' she says.

'Lara?'

Finally she looks at Dad standing there, clumsy and awkward.

'Michel.'

I can see us still standing there as the sun sinks into the sea.

'Oh, come on, guys.' I grab Dad's hand and drag him towards Mum. I pull Mum to her feet, kiss her on the cheek, and position her in front of Dad. 'Where's Fred?'

'There are some steps down to a garden over there,' Mum says, looking at Dad, but talking to me. 'He's with another English boy. There's a climbing frame. Be careful.'

'Your hair looks lovely, Mum.'

She smiles, but I can see how nervous and uncertain she is. She has lost weight and overdone the makeup a little.

'So does yours, Dad,' I add awkwardly. 'I'll go and find Fred then.'

Turning at the top of the steps, I see Dad has taken Mum's hands in his own. I practically float down the huge stone steps.

The lower garden has no grass, there are too many trees. Surrounding the circle of packed earth are several huge flowerpots containing giant ferns. At the far end of the garden is a wooden gate and, beyond that, an alley leading away between the houses.

Fred and a black boy in dark jeans and lime green trainers are on their hands and knees by one of the flowerpots peering at something between them on the ground. I tap Fred on the shoulder. He jumps back, recognises me and gives me a huge grin.

'It just climbed up onto my book by itself,' he signs. 'It's massive.'

A black beetle is slowly crossing the surface of Mars, as depicted on the cover of one of Fred's favourite fantasy books. Fred's fringe is so long I can hardly see his eyes. His t-shirt reads Posh kids make me sick.

''We're busy, do you know what I mean?'

The accent is pure Liverpool, but as soon as the face looks up it is obvious that the English boy is in fact an English girl.

'I'm his sister,' I explain.

'He don't talk much, does he?'

'He's deaf. But he lip reads. He's called Fred. I'm Sam. What's your name?'

'Do you know what this beetle's called?'

'Luigi?'

'Oh, you're cracking me up, that's so funny,' the girl says.

'She said her name was Keisha,' Fred signs.

'What did he say?' the girl asks.

'He said Scousers are sarcastic little gits.' I turn to Fred. 'Dad's here.'

Fred nods but doesn't seem in any rush to meet a man he hasn't seen since he was two years old.

Halfway up the steps I call over my shoulder, 'It's a stag beetle.'

How long do I stand there, staring at my parents sitting there together in the winter sunshine? I have spent most of my life waiting for this moment. I want to race over and hug them both, and lose myself in their arms. At the same time, I am now old enough to recognise that my parents have nine years catching up to do.

It is amazing that Mum is here at all. Both Dad and I convinced ourselves that it would be impossible for us all to meet, that there would be powerful and dangerous forces at work, that Mum would be unable or unwilling to leave England. But we were wrong. Somehow she and Fred are here. Maybe we have become paranoid and imagine threats were there are none. Maybe our troubles really ended with the sinking of the Dauntless off the coast of Lipari.

'Keisha. We're eating.'

It is the loud-shirted man sitting with the older woman who is shouting. The waiter crosses the terrace balancing three enormous pizzas.

Dad leans across and kisses Mum, her face away from me. She resists then reaches out her hand to pull him to her. Below us in the town a clock strikes one, followed by three other clocks in rapid succession.

'Keisha,' the loud-shirted man shouts a second time.

I sit down beside my parents, placing the paper bag containing my chocolate on the floor in the shade.

'Are you still hungry?' Dad asks.

I shake my head. 'I couldn't manage more than three of those pizzas.'

Nobody speaks for a couple of seconds.

'You know when you want something so badly it hurts?' Jump in with both feet, Sam, why don't you?

The look in Mum's eyes is way too intense. I want to ask if she and Fred are joining us on the boat, if we can be a family again.

'We kept all those origami animals you made, Dad,' I say instead, chickening out. 'In a box at the back of the cupboard under the stairs.'

'If anyone is having three pizzas, it's you, Michel,' Mum says, her hand stroking his cheek. 'You're thinner than a coat of paint.'

'Scusami, I interrupt, please.'

It is the hamster-faced hotel manager.

'There is gentleman inside wishing to speak with Sam Blanchard.'

I stand up. 'I'll tell him to go back to the boat and wait.'

'Who?' Mum asks.

'He was meant to be selling the fish and waiting for us at the boat but Rafael just had to gate crash the party. Typical.'

Mum's face registers surprise. I turn to find the hotel manager pointing a mobile phone camera at the three of us.

'I take photo of happy family reunion,' he explains nonchalantly. 'I email later on, yes?'

Which is slightly weird, like what business is it of his to take our photo? But I am more angry about Rafael's appearance at the hotel. Fuming, I follow the hotel manager inside and through to the reception area.

'Sam' says a voice softly behind me. 'What a pleasant surprise.'

I freeze.

9

Vikki Gutner steps out of the airport. It is noticeably cooler in Rome than in Sicily. She crosses the tarmac towards the long stay car park. Pushing the door button on her rental car keys she quickly spots the flashing indicators of the Alfa Giulietta. Red, she hates red.

Forty minutes sleep on the plane was nowhere near enough but it has to do. She tosses her bags onto the back seat and takes her place behind the wheel. The Satnav says the journey to Anzio will take just over an hour, but straight out of the airport she finds herself stuck in traffic. She switches on the radio, flicking through the channels until she finds a Rossini opera, powerful and dramatic. Love and death. She doesn't know much about love, but death …

Her plan is straightforward, find and interrogate the two witnesses who claim to have seen the Blanchards and Rafael Santoni and check any closed circuit television camera footage that has been recorded in the vicinity of the harbour to see if they show the direction the fishing boat was heading in when it left. Assuming she is able to positively identify the boat and its occupants, and Gutner is convinced her analysis is correct, she'll find them. The fugitives are travelling slowly, hopping from small port to small port, hugging the coast and avoiding the open sea.

It shouldn't be that difficult to trace their movements over the last three days unless the sighting in Anzio has been a mistake or a cleverly calculated false trail. In which case she will abandon the hunt and concentrate instead on ensuring that when Watson and Messi catch up with her there will be only one survivor.

10

The suit is two sizes too small and tighter than walrus's bikini. The moustache is longer than I remember and reinforces the walrus theme, with the bruise on his right cheek suggesting an alpha male who has got into too many fights on a wind swept beach in the middle of the southern Atlantic. Only the ponytail confuses the image.

'Like I said when we met, Sam, you're a survivor.' Sven smiles. 'So far.'

'Go to hell. What do you want?'

'I'm here to help. As usual.'

Sven' first act of helping was in Brussels three weeks ago when he barged into a café, impersonated a waiter, and kidnapped Rafael and I.

'A present.' He offers me a small leather backpack.

'I don't want anything from you.'

'OK, they are for Rafa and your father. You call him Rafa now?'

'Get lost.'

'That's a little rude. Without me, your little family reunion wouldn't be happening so I think …'

'Who cares what you think?'

'Oh. Sam. There is a place for anger but right now you need your brains, for want of a better word. I'm here to cut a deal so that everyone wins. You cannot fight the entire world by yourself. Even your paranoid papa understands that.'

The fat hotelier appears, carrying a large bottle of champagne in a bucket and accompanied by a waiter holding a tray upon which are various bowls and four champagne flutes. With a wink and a conspiratorial smile, Sven slings the backpack I have refused back on his shoulder and takes the tray from the waiter. As he does so, his jacket falls open. Only I can see the gun nestling in a holster beneath his armpit.

'Let's join your parents on the terrace. I love surprises, don't you?'

The beaming hotelier nods vigorously.

Mum and Dad pull away from each other as we reach the table. Dad's jaw clenches as we sit down, but he says nothing. Sven makes a show of taking the champagne from the hotelier and untwisting the wire to release the cork, which flies out over the terrace wall to clatter on a rooftop out of sight below.

'Michel, Madame, me and … is Sam old enough to have one?' Sven holds the bottle over the fourth glass. 'Sixteen soon I think. A big girl now.'

One of those moments when you really need deadly superpowers.

'To a happy reunion.' Sven holds his glass up then takes a sip. He places the glass on the table and removes the backpack, which he puts on the ground beside my bag of chocolate.

'How did you survive the explosion on the ship?' Michel asks.

'Yeah, I read about that. Putting your military training to good use.'

Only Sven is drinking. He has a thicker skin than week old custard.

'Do you have any idea how many people are hunting you?' he says. 'You thought the Blanchard family was going to be allowed to disappear with a couple of expensive military assets to play happy families somewhere on a desert island just like that? Wakey, wakey. And, guys, destroying mafia fish pens isn't helping, let's be honest. These are not easy-going people. I hear the navy still want their property back.'

'You cannot own sentient beings, it's called slavery,' I mutter.

Sven gives me a slow handclap. 'I can see why they invited you to speak in the European Parliament. Where were we? Ah.' He starts counting on his fingers, 'The mafia, the military, world religions; believe me, they will hate the idea of human beings not being the chosen ones. Then you have national governments, and multinational corporations; no-one is going to be happy if some brainy fish award themselves tribal rights to oceanic real estate.' Another sip of champagne. 'Did I tell you I bumped into a couple of guys looking for you down in the town? We had a bit of an argument.' He points to the bruise on his cheek. 'You may have heard the sirens. Both dead I'm afraid.'

'What's your point?' Dad says.

'My point is, my friend, that there is no opt out option. You know that as well as I do. You have to strike a deal to survive and it may as well be with me.'

'Go to hell.'

‘We could all be making money. You and your lovely family would be safe. Even the dolphins could be rich: merchandising, innovation, product placements. Where do dolphins keep their credit cards?’ Sven pats his chest as if trying to locate his pockets. ‘All the fish they could swallow. My clients …’

‘Do you care about the planet?’ I say, to shut him up.

Sven makes a show of thinking for a second then shakes his head.

‘But since you do, you could spend your share saving it,’ he says brightly. ‘And so could Dad,’ he adds, patting him on the shoulder.

‘Maybe, if everyone stopped behaving like children ...’ Mum has been staring down at the table since Sven arrived. She looks at Dad and I. ‘The pair of you should listen to Mr …?’

‘My name is not important.’

‘You can’t drag Sam round the Mediterranean forever, Michel. She has school and exams.’

‘This is more important than my exams, Mum.’

‘So let’s hear your plan, Sam,’ Sven says. ‘You go to the UN and make representations to the international emperor of graffiti, Banksie Moon. He will welcome a new nation to the club; something the Palestinians have failed to achieve for decades, but hey. The Republic of Flipperania. Of course, attending the UN could be tricky; Switzerland is landlocked and New York is seven thousand kilometres away.’

A mobile phone starts ringing. ‘Excuse me.’ Sven pulls his mobile out of his jacket pocket. He stands up, crosses the terrace and disappears inside the hotel.

I can’t believe that Mum has sided with Sven. And now she is avoiding my eye. And what does Sven mean when he says that the family reunion is thanks to him?

‘Can you check on Fred please, Sam?’ Mum says, then turns to Dad. ‘We need to order some food, they may stop serving.’ She is trying to make everything feel normal, like she does at home. She is a master of re-direction. Without it the family would have fallen apart when Dad was kidnapped all those years ago. But right now it doesn’t feel like she is holding things together; it feels like she is holding something back.

‘We haven’t even …’ I start.

‘Mum’s right.’ Dad gives me a little nod that says leave this with me.

'Whatever.'

Tell her about the plan, Dad, I think to myself as I walk away. Tell her about France and Carla Biseti. Fred and the girl are sitting on the ground at the foot of the steps. Somewhere close by, a motorbike roars and screeches to a halt. The girl has her hands over her ears and is pretending to shout at Fred. As I squat down beside them, an explosion shatters everything.

11

The world is spinning and I feel sick. Someone shakes me roughly by the shoulder.

Go to hell.

More shaking. I find myself staring into Fred's face. I push him away and sit up. My head is ringing. Two trees have tumbled over from the terrace, their trunks splintered, their crowns now in the garden, scattered oranges all around us. The toppling trees have destroyed the stone balustrade and huge chunks of masonry are strewn about. It is a miracle that neither Fred nor I nor the girl have been injured or killed.

The girl seems to be shouting but no sound is coming from her mouth.

'Keisha's asking if you are going to die,' Fred signs, 'but it's just a cut.'

Fred is lip reading, but why can't I hear Keisha? I feel for my ears, and find them. There is blood in my hair and on my face.

Keisha stands up and starts climbing the steps.

'She's getting you some water.'

In a rush I remember the world beyond the garden and scramble to my feet. I stagger up the stone steps dodging the chunks of masonry and an orange tree branch.

Half the tables have simply vanished. To my right is a foot in a shoe. The large family are nowhere to be seen. Keisha is standing quite still, with her back to me. Beyond her on the ground is a body in a loud shirt.

The back of the hotel is an open wound. The rear entrance has disappeared and part of the rear wall has collapsed to reveal a bed and a bath hanging over a pouting lip of splintered floorboards on the first floor, like a soft toy with its stuffing falling out.

A tree has fallen, blocking my view of the table where Dad and Mum are sitting. I lurch forward, pushing through the branches, ripping my green dress, and burst through the other side, narrowly avoiding stepping into the void; the railing on the edge of the terrace has disappeared.

At first it seems like a miracle has taken place. Mum and Dad have been shielded from the first brutal impact of the blast by the fountain and are both alive. Then I see mum's leg, at an impossible angle. Dad is tying a tourniquet round her thigh and she is lying back, in shock and shaking from the pain. The top of Dad's right ear is partially torn away and his cheek has swollen to almost hide his right eye. His shirt is ripped at the shoulder and oozing blood.

I rush forward and kneel beside them. Dad mouths the words 'it's OK' as he sees me then turns back to mum and gently strokes the side of her face. Her eyes open. She sees my face and looks frightened.

'It's OK, Mum. Just a cut.'

Mum tugs Dad's arm and mutters. Realising that neither of us can hear her, she switches to signing.

'My fault, I shouldn't have come.'

'No. Don't be stupid, Lara,' Dad signs back.

Mum closes her eyes for an instant. 'I led him straight to you. I'm sorry.'

'It's not your fault, it's mine.'

'Go, please go.'

Dad shakes his head. 'Look at me, I can't go anywhere and, besides, I'm not leaving you. Not again, not now, not ever.' He takes Mum's hand in his own.

In that instant I understand that everything is now up to me. Grabbing the leather backpack and the bag of chocolates, I stand up. Within the buzz in my head another sound is emerging, a waving pulsating sound. A siren.

'An ambulance is coming.,' I sign. 'I'm going back to the boat. France, you said, didn't you? Call me on Rafael's mobile phone.'

For a moment it looks like Dad is going to shout at me, to remind me I am still a child, to tell me to sit down and stop being stupid. Then the look in his eyes changes and I know that he trusts me.

'I will call Rafael's phone every six hours,' Dad says. 'But keep the phone switched off and …'

'Never speak for more than fifty seconds.' I parrot back to him the lesson he has taught me, ''and take the batteries out when you're not using it because they can track you even when the phone is switched off.'

He smiles and shows me his watch. We synchronise at seventeen minutes past one. 'Don't let Calypso boss you about, Sam. She thinks of you and Rafael as little more than calves or puppies. Show her you are responsible.

‘Where’s Fred?’ Mum asks, her eyes suddenly wide with alarm.

‘Don’t worry about him. I’ll take him with me.’

Mum glances at Dad. He nods. I kiss them both, heart pounding, and push my way back through the fallen tree before they change their minds.

Fred is standing beside Keisha, staring at the carnage.

‘We have to go,’ I sign.

‘What about her?’

‘I don’t know, Fred. Maybe her relatives will …’

‘Her dad’s right there. He’s dead.’

I pull his arm and drag him away, ‘Come on.’

‘What about Mum?’

‘They’re OK,’ I lie. ‘They’ll join us later.’

We run down the steps, across the lower garden, push open the gate and out into the alley. Fred pulls away, runs back into the garden. He returns with his book, looking up at me, his jaw set, as if defying me to tell him he cannot take it with him.

There is only one rule; take the path that goes down. Right then left. A blur of colour, bright sunshine, deep shadows. The explosion has affected my balance; I tumble headlong onto a narrow strip of flowers beside a back gate, letting go of both bags. The brown paper bag splits, sending my chocolates spinning across the ground.

You do not abandon chocolate.

Fred and I are scooping everything into the backpack when I become aware of someone standing over us. I look up to find Keisha staring down, her lips pressed tightly together, her eyes wet with tears.

I shake my head.

Fred gets up and crosses over to stand beside Keisha, glowering at me defiantly. Behind them is a flash of electric blue. A motorbike. Are we being chased? Shouldering the backpack, I scramble to my feet and pull Fred’s arm, but he is holding Keisha’s and won’t let go. Choices, choices.

‘Come on then,’ I shout. ‘but hurry.’

We sprint away, all three of us. I catch sight of the motorbike again, through an archway slightly below us. The headlight dazzles me briefly as the handlebars turn to face us. The motorbike surges forwards.

Racing back the way we have just come, I take a left turn, the two children hot on my heels. Take the path that goes down towards the sea, I keep telling myself, but it isn't always possible. Round another blind corner, the path leads back up the hill. The escalating buzz in my ears tells me the motorbike is closing on us. My feet skid as I dash into a shorter darker passageway, Fred and Keisha crashing into me from behind. We burst out into another alley twice the width. Long steps heading downward. Do motorbikes do steps? I glance over my shoulder. A blur of electric blue confirms that yes they do.

Dodging into another alley we find ourselves blinded by bright sunshine and wrapped up in washing. We beat our way through sheets, pants, frocks, and pillow cases hanging out to dry and, emerging out the other side, we race forward again only to be brought to a standstill almost immediately.

A dead end. A low railing marks the end of the alley. Beyond it is the sky, a beautiful view of terracotta rooftops below and, beyond them, La Vita Nuova bobbing in the harbour beside the shimmering sea. Bouncing off the narrow walls of the alley, the roar of the approaching motorbike is audible even to my damaged ears. I have blown it. I push the children into the nearest doorway, all we can do is hope that the biker won't have seen the direction we took, but it is unlikely. Overriding the panic, the pain and the fear is anger. I am running away from the very thing I have been dreaming of for over half my life. How have I been so stupid as to believe we could simply meet up and play happy families?

The washing that hangs across the alley becomes a shaking mess of colours lunging towards us at high speed. We press ourselves back against the door. The laundry billows and slows then, as if something has snapped, suddenly everything is surging forwards again. I catch a glimpse of electric blue and a face with dark eyebrows in an orange helmet as the motorbike passes us and smacks into the low railing to our left, catapulting the rider high into the air out over the rooftops, the washing lines wrapped around his chest and trailing coloured laundry behind him like the tail beneath a kite.

I guess he screams as he falls, but I can't barely hear the roaring motorbike engine on its side in the alley in front of us.. Fred and Keisha step forward to stare out over the rooftops, jaws open.

'No time for that.' I grab the pair of them and steer them back to the alley with the steps. We race down. Soon the alley becomes less steep and we reach a narrow street. Left or right? We turn right and hurry towards a bunch of tourists in big brimmed hats, fingering postcards hanging outside a shop.

An old couple look up as we approach. The shock in their faces is clear as they register my ripped dress, blood streaming down my face. The man puts out his arms to try to catch me. I push him aside and he loses his balance. A row of dresses outside a shop tumbles over with him.

One street leads to another until finally the road is level. We must be down by the harbour. More people gawping. A group of Chinese tourists are taking photos of a little fountain set against a wall in the shade. I barge past, cup my hands beneath one of the stone fish mouths and collect cool water and splash it across my face. The crystal clear water in the carved stone basin turns a cloudy red. I lean forwards and drink directly from the fish's mouth. My hair is matted with blood but that will have to wait. The children find metal bowls hanging on chains and are drinking beside me. We bow for the assembled nosy tourists and hurry away. A moment later we find the sea and the harbour.

Rafael appears from the cabin as I skid to a halt in front of La Vita Nuova. He looks as shocked as the tourists. I struggle to catch my breath.

'What happened?' I see him say.

'An explosion at the hotel. My parents are both injured.'

Can he hear me? Am I actually making any noise?

Rafael points behind me and says something I can't hear.

'What?'

He points again.

'Oh, that's Fred and his friend Keisha.'

12

As we pull away from the small harbour I back stare at the plume of smoke hanging over the hill and the town. The Big Event I have been waiting over nine years to see is over. Instead of us all being reunited, the Blanchard family has been torn apart again, children one way, adults the other.

We have travelled an hour away from the port, skirting the western edge of Elba then heading north, by the time Calypso shows her face. She immediately understands that something is wrong. Rafael cuts the engines and grabs the hydrophone and laptop, while I sign what had happened. I cannot hear their clicks at all. Fred and the girl are hanging over the side of the boat, their eyes big as doughnuts.

'Can I talk with them?' Fred keeps asking. 'Do they really understand?'

'Who are the calves?' Calypso asks.

'My brother and a girl whose family were killed in the town,' I sign.

'Her name is Keisha,' Fred signs, spelling out the letters of her name, having decided that if I can sign to dolphins then so can he.

'Where is Michel?' Calypso asks.

'In town, with Mum,' I answer. 'Is Steve here? We must get away from Italy and the mafia. Dad said we should go to France.'

Rafael taps my shoulder and he gestures that he can't understand. I shout the words out as best I can.

Rafael says something I cannot hear.

'He doesn't think that there is enough petrol,' Fred says, having lip read.

'Well go and check,' I shout at the top of my voice.

Rafael gives me a dark look then leaves.

'Is he your boyfriend?' Keisha asks, via Fred. She hasn't said much to me since she got on the boat and the few words she has said have all been rude or sarcastic.

'Tell her it's none of her business. And go inside, both of you, it's dangerous out here.'

Keisha says something to Fred. They look at me and laugh and disappear inside.

'Careful with the calves,' Calypso advises on the laptop display. 'You are all stressed.'

'Where's Steve?'

'Not far. When he arrives we need to talk.'

Rafael powers up the engines and sets off. I stay on deck, not interested in having company. Calypso hangs around on the surface close to the boat for a while then drifts away.

Over the course of an hour and a half, my hearing begins to return, like the sun burning the mist off fields on a crisp autumn morning. First I notice the rumble of the engines, a door banging, a shriek followed by a wave of laughter. The buzzing in my head has shifted. When I cover my ears half the noise disappears, I must be hearing the wash of the sea against the boat.

I worry about my parents. Have they found a hospital? Are they operating on Mum? Is Dad there with her?

Only the thin line of clouds gives any hint of the existence of land, over the horizon now and way behind us. We are alone at sea; me, Rafael, a couple of kids, two weird sea creatures, and a small boat.

Get out of that, Sam.

Calypso is up alongside again, but still no sign of Steve. I go inside.

'Ooo, where's my boyfriend?' Keisha says, looking at me while she flutters her eyelashes.

The door hasn't clicked in the lock and already she is giving me grief. She and Fred are sitting at the table in the galley playing cards and laughing. Why did I agree to take her?

'Do you know how deep the sea is out here?" I say.

'Is it as deep as your love?' she fires back. 'Nice sacks by the way.'

'Nice what?'

'Sacks.' She points up and down at my clothes. 'Yer clothes. They're boss.'

My dress is crumpled and blood stained.

'Can you control the girl, please?' I sign to Fred.

'Her name is Keisha,' he signs back.

'It's rude making signs,' says Keisha. 'Has no-one told you?'

Rafael appears from down below.

'We do have enough fuel but …" he starts.

'We need to go north,' I cut him off mid-sentence. 'Closer to land.'

'We are safer out here where no-one can see us.'

Though I no longer believe we are safe anywhere I keep my mouth shut.

'Do you think they kiss?' Keisha says to Fred.

'Will you shut up,' I shout, 'or do I have to tie you up and put you outside?'

'There's laws against that. Child abuse and everything. I have my rights, you know.' Tears are welling up as Keisha stands up, dropping her playing cards on the table. The cabin door bangs shut behind her. I find some jeans and a fleece, and squeeze into the tiny bathroom to change and to wash my face and hair.

13

Keisha is at the back of the boat staring blindly out to sea. I approach softly and sit down on the deck beside her. Me and mini me; how many times over the past ten days has Dad come and rescued me from my demons as I have sulked in exactly the same spot?

If she is aware of me, she isn't letting on. Every now and then her jaw clenches and unclenches but aside from that she might be in hibernation.

Close your eyes and you can pretend you are anywhere, cocooned in the hum of the engine and the white noise of the sea. I imagine that I am back at home, lying in bed staring up at the ceiling, watching the wind blown shifting shadows of the branches of the cherry tree that grows in the front garden by the orange streetlight. I open my eyes.

'I bet your Dad was a really cool guy,' I say.

Nothing.

'Did he have a strong Italian accent? Mine does. A French accent, that is, even though he's lived in England for nearly twenty years.'

Listen to yourself, Sam, nearly half that time he wasn't in England at all, but she doesn't need to know that. Too much information.

Keisha sighs.

'They both looked so happy in the hotel garden.' I try a different tack. 'Was the old lady …'

'He's an idiot, stupid as a bar of soap.'

'Want some chocolate?'

A mumbled response I cannot hear.

'You have to talk louder, my ears are still ringing from the explosion.'

'I said, how old are you?' she shouts. 'Are you deaf like yer meff brother?'

Count to ten, Sam. No hitting ten year olds.

'I'm sixteen tomorrow.'

'We're all going to die. You know that, don't you?' she says, grabbing the chocolate out of my hand.

'Was she your grandmother? The old lady with the orange hair?'

'Shurrup. Who cares about the old bag? She doesn't like black kids, anyway. She don't say nothing but you can tell, do you know what I mean? You're doing me head in. It's all right fer posh gits like you, with yer big boats, and yer stacks of money.'

'This isn't our boat. We borrowed it to escape a few weeks ago … OK, we stole it, actually.'

'Oh great.' She turns to look at me. 'I've joined a bunch of pirates and now the bizzies are after us and …'

'Bizzies?' I push my windswept hair out of my face.

'The lads in blue. The police.'

'It's worse than that, Kid. Everyone is after us. The police, the army, the mafia …'

'Nice. Me Dad said he was taking us on a quiet holiday to meet me granny and now I'm on the most wanted list. Brilliant. He's as much …' She stops mid-sentence, overwhelmed by emotion.

I wait then reach out a hand. Her sobs are shaking her skinny shoulders as I draw her gently towards me. Fat tears rolling down our stupid faces, studying in minute detail that flaking paintwork on the gunwale, lost in our little worlds, mourning the past and dreading the future.

'Was that yer mum and Dad up there in the garden?'

I nod.

'Are they dead too?'

I shake my head. 'They're both injured but I think … I'm hoping …'

Keisha puts her hand on my arm and smiles. 'They'll take her down the ozzie and patch her up. Sorted.'

My expression gives me away.

'The hospital,' Keisha explains. 'Don't you southerners know nothing?'

'I'm from Yorkshire. That's east of Liverpool, not south.'

Keisha does a wide-eyed la-di-da expression and we both laugh then sit there side by side staring out at nothing in particular, of which there is plenty, endless waves on an endless sea beneath the endless sky.

'That thing with the dolphin, that's just a trick right?'

'What?'

'Fred really believed it were talking, didn't he? He's a nice kid but kinda soft, you know what I mean?'

'If you mean he's stupid, then no,' I answer. 'He's deaf, that's all.'

‘I suppose it doesn’t matter what noises the dolphin makes.’ Keisha fiddles with the laces of her trainers. ‘You just have all the stuff they’re meant to be saying stored on the computer. To fool people. Like a party trick to earn some money, eh?’

I don’t have the energy to explain it all.

‘Something like that,’ I agree.

‘I knew it,’ she says, eyes gleaming. ‘I’m not daft, you know. I could see it was just a trick.’

‘Are you all right?’

Rafael is standing behind us.

‘You need to come inside,’ he says. ‘The hydrophones are picking a lot of noise. Steve’s back. It sounds like they’re arguing somewhere under the boat.

He studies our faces and seems to be on the verge of saying something.

‘Don’t even start,’ I say.

Rafael shrugs and disappears back inside.

‘Our resident therapist, Captain Skinny,’ I explain to Keisha, as I wipe my face. ‘He is so emotionally sensitive that he has his own TV show and the United Nations send him to conflict zones to end wars.’

‘I heard that,’ Rafael’s voice drifts out through the open cabin door.

‘Can he cook fish fingers?’ Keisha asks, as we climb to our feet. ‘He’s all gooey eyed for you, isn’t he?’ She puts a hand over her heart and pretends to swoon. ‘True lurve, oh yeah.’

Kids.

14

'I need someone to move all the food that is out on deck and bring it inside, in case it rains,' Rafael says. 'There's a sack of rice, potatoes, onions, some tins and bread. Are you kids strong enough to lift stuff? Even just the little things and then …'

'Don't be soft,' Keisha cuts in. 'I'm stronger than you any day. I carry everything in me dad's restaurant, me. Not skinny like you, even if you do have hands the size of bin lids.'

She prods Fred who is sitting on the floor reading his book. 'Gerrup, there's work to do, soldier,' she says.

The two younger ones step out on deck. In the background the clicks and whistles of the dolphins are pouring out of the laptop's speaker.

'We've got a problem,' Rafael says, adjusting our course. 'The translation software is only catching fragments but I think Steve and Calypso are fighting over where to go.'

'But we've already decided …'

'We haven't done anything. You just came back and announced that we had to go to France.'

'That's what Dad …'

'Michel isn't here, Sam. There's just you, me, Calypso and Steve.'

'They can't decide.'

'Because they're dolphins? You assume it is the humans who decide?'

'Because we know …'

'We know what?' Rafael cuts me off. 'We know what exactly?'

He's right. I have no idea where we will find safety. The cabin door bangs open. Fred and Keisha come in, bums first, dragging a huge sack.

'Where do you want the tatties?' Keisha calls over her shoulder.

'Wherever there's space,' I answer.

'We need a plan. In me dad's kitchen we always …'

'Was your dad a chef?'

She stops dragging and straightened up. For a moment she looks like she wants to hit me.

'It's still his kitchen, even if he is dead.' Keisha grabs Fred's arm and pulls him back towards the cabin door. 'By the way,' she shouts as the door is closing, 'those dolphins are making a right racket.'

'Did Michel say exactly where we should go?'

I shake my head. 'France, that's all he said.'

Rafael pulls open the drawer by the wheel and shows me the GPS. About the size of a book, it looks more complicated than the satnavs in cars. There are buttons all round the sides for a start. The only thing Rafael loves more than gadgets is the opportunity to show off how much he knows about them. He starts explaining what the various buttons do but, since the machine is switched off, and since I am not really interested, it's in one ear out the other.

'If I switch it on, it has to be off again in less than ninety seconds in case ...'

'Yeah, yeah,' I say. 'Seen the film, got the t-shirt.'

Before we can argue, the cabin door opens. Keisha and Fred drag in another load of food and I pick up the laptop and head outside.

It is getting colder and the water is choppy. Rafael and I are used to it by now but if things get worse I can see the kids throwing up all night. Two dolphin backs break the surface ten metres from the boat. I turn up the volume on the laptop. The speaker crackles and the air is full of dolphin sounds. It is comforting hearing the clicks and whistles. When they are communicating to each other, Calypso and Steve make no attempt to slow or lower the pitch of their sounds to human hearing range, why would they. As a result, little if any of their conversation is translated.

Rafael comes out and joins me and we wait patiently, watching and listening. A dozen seagulls fly over, heading towards the coast that has long since disappeared over the horizon.

'Sam. Sam,' appears on the laptop screen.

That much I do understand. I wait for someone to surface.

'We have to go back.' Steve.

'Let me explain to them.' Calypso.

'Make them listen.' Steve.

We can hear the dolphins but we still cannot see either of them. We walk round to the back of the boat. Behind us Fred and Keisha are still popping in and out, hauling food inside. Keisha's voice more than makes up for Fred's silence; Boy can that one talk, as my mum would say.

Calypso surfaces first.

'What's in the bag? It's boss. Can I have it?'

I spin round. Keisha is holding the small leather rucksack Sven gave me.

'Just take it inside, put it on the table and leave it alone. Find yourselves something to eat.'

'Whatever we like?'

'Whatever you like.'

One of the most annoying things about dolphins is the fact that their faces, unlike the faces of ten-year-old girls who have just been told that they can eat what they like, don't show emotions. You get that same big dumb smile but that's all you get. I'm really happy. Smile. I'm angry. Smile. I'm confused. Smile. I'm sad, frightened, scheming, bored, serious, hungry, pissed off … smile, smile, smile.

Calypso is smiling. 'I have bad news,' she says.

We are low on fuel, floating in a stolen boat in the middle of the Mediterranean. My parents are lying injured somewhere. We have more enemies than a politician on I'm a Celebrity, we are lumbered with a couple of goofy kids, and stuck with two stroppy talking dolphins. What can Calypso possibly add that could be marked down as bad news?

'Let's suppose that I want to hear more bad news,' I sign.

Still smiling. 'We have to go back to the fish pens.'

Rafael and I look at each other.

'Why?' he says.

Which sums it up nicely, I decide as I pass the message on to Calypso and Steve.

'The sixth pen,' Calypso says. 'It doesn't contain tuna. There are trapped dolphins in it.'

I shake my head. 'We have too many troubles already.'

'They will sell them to an army or to a zoo.'

'Not our problem,' I shout with my hands, making vicious and expansive gestures.

'There are four dolphins. Two are injured. One is just a calf.'

Steve pops up. 'Humans care only about things, not sea beings. Forget them, we can do this alone.'

Sea beings as opposed to land beings, which is us humans.

'The island is over sixty kilometres south by now,' Rafael says beside me. 'It would take three or four hours. In the wrong direction. And then there's the fuel.'

Through the cabin window I see Fred and Keisha sword fighting with sticks of celery. Little kids playing, oblivious of danger.

'Sam.' Calypso calls. 'There is something else I must tell you both.'

I take a deep breath and ignore the clicks behind me.

Rafael touches my sleeve. 'We have to listen,' he says quietly.

'Steve couldn't talk with them, but I could, a little, and I …' Calypso says.

'Why couldn't he?'

'When Steve was captured he was only a few months old. He has no memory of his pod or his mother. For me it was different.' Calypso disappears beneath the waves but the hydrophone carries on picking up her voice. 'When we reached the fish pen one of the captured dolphins swam towards us and she saw me.'

She pops up again beside the boat.

'Why didn't you say something before? When did you discover all this?'

'We tried to tell Michel this morning. He wouldn't listen. The dolphins in the net are from my pod.'

'How could you know that? Did you recognise them?'

'No, but she called me by my mother's name. We are going back.'

With that she turns and heads south. Her dorsal fin breaks the surface of the waves four or five times. The last time she surfaces a second dorsal fin appears alongside hers, about thirty metres from the boat, then they are gone.

Rafael and I look at each other. I kick the gunwale. We can't head for France alone; we have no choice.

15

'This is all you have?'

'What were you expecting, Honey? A fleet of flying Ferraris? Father Christmas in his Popemobile? If we'd known a big shot from Sicily was coming to Anzio to look at our harbour parking, I'd have organised something special.'

The parking supervisor, boots up on his desk, pushes his lank greasy hair out of his eyes for the tenth time and flashes his sarcastic smile. He is as untidy as his sweaty little office, with its broken chairs and its acrid smell of burnt coffee.

Vikki Gutner glances through the dirty window at the parked cars and the masts of the boats. She stands up and picks her briefcase up off the floor.

'Maybe the supermarket car parks have interesting shots of mums trying to reverse into parking spaces while …'

He doesn't finish his sentence. Swinging her case, Gutner swipes his fat boots off his desk and, as he loses balance, she smashes the case into the side of his head sending him crashing to the floor. The man howls, clutching his ear. The back of his chair falls off and clatters down beside him.

'There is a video camera mounted on the lamp post at the end of the harbour car park facing the last ten spaces and the open sea,' Gutner says quietly, standing over the man. 'Could I see that footage, please? Same as before, three days ago around three pm.'

'OK, OK. No need for violence.'

It is Gutner's turn to smile. 'If there was no need for violence, my briefcase wouldn't be covered in dents and scratches. I don't have as much time to waste as you have.'

16

'It's more difficult at night,' Rafael insists.

'Nothing gets past you, does it?' I reply.

'Please go outside and check we are safe,' he says patiently, switching on the underwater lights.

Check we are safe? We are as safe as bungee jumpers standing on top of a bridge tied to ropes made of strands of spaghetti stapled end to end.

Within three hours of leaving Elba, thanks to two obstinate dolphins, we are heading straight back into the jaws of the dragon.

You couldn't create a better example of the downside of intelligence. If Calypso and Steve were dogs we could attach a lead to their collars and drag them north. Instead it is Calypso calling all the shots and Rafael and I on the leads. Dad warned me. He is able to reason with Calypso, adult to adult, but Calypso calls our bluff, knowing that we have to stay together and seeing Rafael and I for what we are, a couple of useless teenager donks.

Night has fallen as the island was appearing up ahead, a jagged black silhouette wedged between an indigo star-splashed sky and the fragmentary moonlight reflecting on the surface of the sea. Rain clouds are sweeping in behind us from the north; the weather is turning for the worse.

By the time we reach the cove, the clouds have overtaken us and the stars have disappeared. Without Dad here, we are nervous. Twice we approach the entrance to the cove only to be forced back when submerged rocks find the bottom of the boat and sharp edges scrape the hull, howling like fingernails along a blackboard. At our third attempt, we find the gap and, moments later, drop anchor in the shelter of the cove.

Fred and Keisha are sprawled out along the benches in the galley, having each eaten a mountain of pasta that Keisha cooked. Not bad for a nine-year-old. Beneath the blankets I found for them in the hold, Fred is snoring gently.

The air outside is chilly. With no moon, the darkness thick and heavy, it is like being underwater already. I shiver.

Rafael cuts the engine and joins me on deck to set up the hydrophone. Gentle lapping waves kiss the beach and slap the sides of the boat.

'There is the path, over there.' I point towards the rocks to our left.

'We must go quickly,' says the laptop, identifying Calypso as the speaker.

'First we are going up the hill to check the layout of the pens from above. It will take twenty minutes. I don't give a stuff what Calypso thinks'.

'Why bother climbing the hill?' says Rafael. 'It's too dark and besides the fish pens are three hundred metres from the shore. You won't see anything.'

'Don't you start. Besides, you are wrong,' I pull the small leather rucksack towards me. I open it and extract the night vision binoculars. 'There's other stuff as well.'

Rafael takes the rucksack and peers inside. His eyes light up then he looks at me questioningly.

'Sven. He was at the hotel. At first I thought he was responsible for the explosion. Now I'm not so sure.'

'Why didn't you tell me?' Rafael says, producing a couple of memory sticks and a Perspex box containing what resembles a toy dragonfly from the rucksack. 'Do you know what is on these?'

'I forgot,' I confess. 'And no, I have no idea.'

Calypso is still staring up at us.

'I said twenty minutes.' I stare straight back at her

'Hurry.'

I watch her sink beneath the surface of the water. I am happy to wind her up. OK, it is childish, but I want to make the most of my few remaining hours as a fifteen year old. Putting the memory sticks back in the rucksack as Rafael pulls out what I know to be a remote control unit, I decide to wake the children.

They take some shaking. Keisha rubs her eyes when she hears the buzzing noise outside. What she sees through the open doorway has her on her feet in seconds, tugging Fred's sleeve and dragging him out on deck.

'Wow, that's that?' she asks.

Hovering in front of her nose is the dragonfly, mechanical wings beating like the real thing. Remote control unit in hand, Rafael gently tweaks the joysticks sending the dragonfly above her head, round Fred and back to its original position. He turns the remote control round so that Keisha can see that on the display screen is the image of her nose in dramatic close up.

‘It can film people’s bogeys?’ she beams.

Rafael nods.

‘Amazing.’

Rafael’s ability to control the tiny drone is not a miracle or a sign of his genius. Sven gave us an identical device three weeks ago when we first met him in Brussels and Rafael, who already knew how to fly remote controlled helicopters, has taken to the dragonfly drone like airheads take to celebrity gossip. Before we lost it, the first miniature drone saved our lives by giving us an eye in the sky when we needed one.

‘Do you trust him?’

‘Who?’

‘What is Sven doing? Why has he given us this?’

‘I don’t know. Come on, put it back in the backpack, we have work to do.’

But Fred has grabbed the backpack and found something more interesting than dragonfly drones. Grinning from ear to ear, he waves a fistful of chocolates at the rest of us.

‘They’re mine,’ I sign.

Fred shakes his head. ‘Finders keepers.’

I throw myself at him. Well you would, wouldn’t you?

‘Guys, it’s not a good time for a private family scenario,’ Rafael says, watching Fred and me locked in a death struggle on the floor, chocolate flying in all directions. ‘Let’s show dignity and fairplay. Can we share it out?’

‘Oh wow, Maltesers, Yay!’ Keisha waves the packet in my face.

‘Leave them, they’re mine,’ I shout.

‘Ooooh!’

A little while later we have finally all calmed down (OK, I have finally calmed down) and the chocolates are back in the backpack except for one bar, which has been broken into equal portions and bolted down faster than a seal swallows fish. A solemn pledge has been made that we will share the rest out later, on pain of agonising death, and four humans are heading up the steep and narrow path that leads up onto the island.

We took the same path two days ago, when we first checked out the fish pens, but that was in daylight and with my dad rather than with the young ones. Negotiating the loose rocks and stones is very different in the dark. I am in the rear and twice I have to catch Keisha as she stumbles close to the edge of the drop. Eventually we reach the top of the path and stand side by side some twenty metres above the cove.

'This way,' I point.

The ground continues to rise but less steeply than before. Some five minutes later, having passed a derelict house with no roof, we reach the crest of the hill. Before us lies the bay with the fish pens. It is so dark that there is barely a reflection off the surface of the water. We drop to our knees and crawl forwards. An owl hoots, scaring us all half to death.

The night-vision binoculars see what our eyes cannot see.

The island is thirty kilometres from the Italian mainland so the mafia gangs feel that they can operate with impunity. According to Rafael, many of these small islands have been used as prisons in the past because of their remoteness. No doubt there are satellites that can spot the pens but the gangs count on there not being the political will to stop their illegal operations and it seems that they have judged correctly.

The six pens are still there in the bay, but where yesterday there were three large boats now there is only one, and that is in darkness.

Are they boats or ships? Rafael has told me that the difference is that a boat can fit on a ship but a ship cannot fit on a boat. Which is weird because you only ever hear of ships in bottles not boats in bottles. So if it is small enough to fit in a bottle it is a ship but if you put a ship in a bottle into a rowing boat then the ship has to become a boat because it is now …

'Are you actually using those binoculars?' Rafael asks.

I ignore him. From above, there is no sign of the damage we did beneath the surface last night. The furthest pen is larger than the others. At the surface it is kept afloat by not one but three concentric rings of thick sealed pipes. Sticking up from the brackets that hold these rings together every couple of metres are posts that support a handrail that also runs right round the pen. Sixty eight posts in all. If they are each two metres apart that makes a circumference of 130 metres, divided by 3.142 … the pen is around forty meters in diameter. My GSCE maths has served a practical purpose for the first time ever. Since you ask, yes, it feels good.

Fred tugs at my sleeve, 'let me see.'

I pass him the binoculars and he passes them in turn to Keisha.

'Do you think it's safe?' I ask Rafael.

Rafael shrugs. 'How many people are left down there?'

'Don't know.'

Rafael takes the binoculars from Keisha and peers through them. Dropping them from his eyes, he fiddles with the various buttons and looks through them a second time. 'Yes, that's better.'

'What?'

'There's one guy in the cabin.' He hands me the binoculars. 'I've switched on the infrared laser; it shows heat instead of light.'

'Tech head.'

He is right though. I now see a pair of white legs glowing in a dark blue darkness, there is clearly someone sitting beyond the open door. We watch and wait but there is no sign of anyone else.

I turn to the kids. 'So, you know what to do?' I pass them the bag I have been carrying.

They nod, we synchronise watches, and Rafael and I shuffle backwards until it is safe to stand without being spotted from the sea. We take the path back to the boat as quickly as the shifting rocks allow. In no time we are crawling into our dry suits and gathering our equipment.

Catching myself in the mirror beside the sink, I stop and take a good look at my fifteen year old face; the dark monobrow, the thatch of thick dark hair. In less than three hours the clock will strike midnight on its never-ending one-way journey through time and I will be sixteen.

In a few weeks my life has been transformed. It now seems normal not to be going to school, not to be living in a house, not to be spending time chatting with friends on the internet while I watch some mindless television adventures series where kids stand in front of green fabric and pretend to be in danger deep in space or halfway up a mountain or in the sea while, behind the camera, their mum or agent holds a drink and a sandwich.

I think of my friend Alex for the first time in ages. What is she doing? Revising, as usual … My GCSEs! Will I even been allowed to sit them? Since I have done no schoolwork for nearly a month I will surely fail them even if, by some weird miracle, everything returns to normal and I find myself sitting at a desk in a quiet hall with a bunch of pens and pencils in a few months …

'Sam. Sam?' Rafael's face appears beside mine in the mirror.

'Do you have exams this summer?' I ask.

'What? Grab the scuba gear. I've set up the iPad, the earphones should have a range of thirty metres.'

I cram a set of earphones into my ears, and shove my hair into the hood of my dry suit. I resemble a seal. We laugh at each other, it is the sound of jangling nerves and fear. Will I even reach my sixteenth birthday?

17

Up on the hill overlooking the bay, Fred and Keisha have completed their first task and can now only wait. Fred has taken pen and notepad to help him communicate with Keisha. They have tried using the infrared binoculars to help Fred lip read in the near total darkness but since it means that Keisha keeps having to move away six metres before Fred can get her in focus, and since Keisha can't lip read, and since they only have one pair of binoculars, it is a rubbish plan1 and quickly abandoned.

They lie side by side propped up on their elbows. Fred has a single LED torch on his small Swiss army penknife and, using a hand to stop any light spilling beyond the sheet of paper, they converse on paper.

Another twenty minutes to wait, Fred scribbles.

Are you scared of the dark? Keisha scribbles back.

No, are you?

Course not.

Fred picks up the binoculars to check the boat. Nothing has changed and no-one has moved. Keisha takes the binoculars from him and peers down into the bay. She flinches.

Fred presses the button on his penknife and lights up her face for a second.

'The boat,' she whispers.

Fred grabs back the binoculars.

In a couple of seconds everything has changed. There isn't one man on the boat, there are at least three. Worse still, two of the men are lowering a dinghy into the water, their bodies glowing bright yellow against the purple water in the thermal image. One man climbs down into the dinghy then collects oars, a large bag and a rifle from the second man still up on deck. Fred pans the binoculars back towards the cabin at the front of the boat. There, through the open doorway, are two legs as before. By the time Fred pans back to the dinghy it has moved off, with both men aboard.

Keisha is tugging at Fred's sleeve. He puts down the binoculars and scribbles what he has seen onto the notepad.

Where are they going? Keisha scribbles back.

Fred puts the binoculars back to his eyes. The dinghy has passed the nearer fish pens and is heading away from them towards the sixth pen.

They know Sam and Rafael are coming, Fred scribbles, so fast he can barely read his own writing. We have to stop them.

Together they race back to the top of the path that leads down to the cove, arriving as the moon emerges through a break in the clouds. Way below them is the last thing they want to see. The dolphins, Sam and Rafael are already out in open sea, swimming away from the cove. The two children jump up and down, waving their arms about, but can only watch as Sam and Rafael disappear beneath the surface of the waves. They are too late.

18

It is pitch black. I am being shaken in all directions, arm and fingers aching as I cling to Calypso's dorsal fin. Ears overloaded by the sound of rushing rippling water, weird whistles and clicks, and the in/out rasping of air that is keeping me alive. And I am angry that we are here at all.

Get it over with and get out.

Totally reliant on Calypso's echolocation to get us to the nets, I barely know which way is up and I haven't seen Rafael for over four minutes.

Calypso slows abruptly. I lurch forwards over her back, the momentum of my dive tanks rolling me headfirst. Disorientated, I come to a stop and find myself face to face with Rafael who is holding a torch. His hand over the beam, leaving only a pencil thin slither of light, he lights my face and then his own.

'Our friends are nervous,' the voice translator says in my earphone.

Is Calypso talking to us or about us?

'While we were waiting, we came to the pen. One female is sick. The male is injured.'

Great. Not only are we risking our necks returning to a mafia operation we raided only yesterday, now we will be escaping at the speed of sea slugs. Still, Rafael's kit is working, we can now hear and understand the dolphins. Rafael moves the beam to light his hand and makes an 'O' with his thumb and index finger. OK?

Grabbing his arm, I turn the torch towards me. As the beam moves it lights the net and then a large white object hanging in the water just inches from my face. I throw myself back, adrenalin pumping so hard that I fear my body will explode.

A plastic bag.

My fear flashes to anger. What is human rubbish doing in the sea? What is wrong with us? I grab the bag, twist it and tie it round my belt then, still fuming, return Rafael's OK. Calypso and Steve are hanging in the water beside us. They offer no comment on the plastic bag. They have seen it all before.

'Where is the ship?' I sign, cupping my hands together to form the prow of a boat.

Calypso points her beak towards her left.

I check my dive computer. Time twenty two thirty two, sea temperature fifteen degrees, depth fifteen metres. We are on time. I give a thumbs up and head towards the surface.

I keep the net at my back. Fewer surprises that way. As we near the surface the light increases a little. I can just make out a small pontoon stuck to the side of the floating pipes that support the nets. A metre below the waves I form another 'O' with my finger and thumb. Rafael nods and we break the surface together.

The mafia ship is straight ahead, maybe thirty metres away, but our eyes aren't drawn by the ship. High on the hill overlooking the bay a fire is burning. As we watch, the fire grows rapidly, its flames licking small bushes, enveloping a tree, its silhouette dark against the bright yellows and oranges of the flames. Fred and Keisha have done exactly as I hoped. Whatever else the man on the ship is doing he is not looking in our direction. For a few minutes at least we can work in relative safety.

I am still congratulating myself on a great plan well executed when I am grabbed from behind in an arm lock around my neck. Before I can react I feel myself lifted out of the water. In my peripheral vision, I see that Rafael is also being attacked. Spitting out my mouthpiece, I try to pull the arm away from my neck before I choke to death but my assailant is far too strong. With one arm he hauls me backwards, scuba kit and all, until my backside is resting on the net's perimeter rings. The pressure on my neck still crushing my windpipe, I am dragged toward what I now realise is a dinghy and not a pontoon. I draw up my right leg, my fumbling fingers clawing at the release catch on the sheath holding my dive knife, but I am already so dizzy with lack of air that I cannot operate the release mechanism.

My attacker's strength is overwhelming. He rocks back and, straightening his legs, lifts me up further out of the water then throws me forwards into the dinghy. The relaxing of the pressure on my throat allows me to drag in a lungful of air as I fall. Slamming hard against the bottom of the dinghy, I see my assailant for the first time. A huge thickset man with a big nose and short cropped hair towers above me, with hands even larger than Rafael's. His ugly smile tells me two things; he has several teeth missing and he enjoys his work.

Struggling with another huge thug about four metres away to my right, Rafael somehow manages to throw himself forwards and, in one movement, the thug flies over his head into the water and the pair of them disappear beneath the waves.

I am still fumbling for my knife as my assailant lets go of the handrail around the fish pen and takes a step towards joining me in the dinghy.

You know how time sometimes stops altogether, or slows down to the point where you can see individual droplets of splashing water crawl through the air like snails climbing a lettuce leaf? No? Well I do. As the man jumps down into the dinghy, time takes a hike. Everything is suddenly happening in a different universe far far away, I watch a heavy boot hang in the air in slow motion, anticipating a moment in a distant future when hard heel connects with soft face, pushing it into the inflated sidewall of the dinghy, distorting it, breaking it. I consider the crunching pain that awaits me at the end of this silent tunnel of anticipation, and the blackness of unconsciousness that will envelop me.

And then in the void where time stands still something amazing happens. Defying the frozen moment, a dark grey shape surges into my field of view, rising up to meet the man with the boot, like a huge living bullet fired from the sea itself. As the man moves incrementally towards me, the grey bullet rises out of the water surrounded by a halo of luminous water drops and although time has stretched to the point of stillness and although the man can see how everything that he expects to happen will not now happen, he is powerless to change anything.

Time snaps back like a spring and in a blink Calypso's beak has smashed into the man's belly crashing him backwards into one of the posts where he smacks his head and, unconscious, bounces forward briefly before dropping back with a thump onto the thick pipes that support the fish pen. Before the man's head hits the pipes Calypso's body is already back in the sea, her flukes disappearing into the water.

Throat burning, I look around and see beside me in the dinghy a length of nylon rope. I grab it and leap up, lashing the man's hands together behind his back. My mouthpiece back in my mouth, I drop back into the water.

19

The adrenaline is pumping. No fear, only anger and the determination to find Rafael, rescue the captured dolphins, and get away as quickly as possible. Whatever it takes.

Heading down, I blow through my nose to clear the water out of my goggles. No sign of Rafael, but it is so dark I could swim straight past Snow White and the Seven Dwarves without seeing them. I feel for the dive light strapped to my thigh, re-strap it over the back of my hand and switch it from flood to spot mode.

They are four metres or so beneath me. Rafael must have tried to escape by diving down, with his attacker somehow holding on to a leg or a foot. It is madness. They have been underwater for about thirty seconds. Rafael, with his diving gear, is able to breathe but the thug clawing at him can only have a few more seconds of air. As I swim down towards them two things happen simultaneously and one of those things is undoubtedly my fault.

By lighting the scene with my torch I have enabled Rafael's attacker to see him. The man reaches out, grabs Rafael's mouthpiece and air pipes and rips them out. Not just out of Rafael's mouth, he rips them away from the scuba tanks altogether. With the pipes hanging from his hand like a wounded octopus the man starts to rise to the surface, leaving Rafael hanging in the water.

The second thing that happens involves the silky grey blur that shoots forwards and smacks into the attacker's kidneys. The man jerks backward. Two seconds later Steve speeds in again, thumping into the attacker's belly, causing the man to fall back into the darkness beyond my torch beam.

A stream of bubbles escapes from Rafael's mouth. My flippers are beating so hard my ankles could snap. Drawing level I take a huge lungful of air then spit my mouthpiece out and press it against Rafael's mouth. Breathe, breathe, I mouth at him, but his eyes stare blankly back at me. I stuff the regulator back in my mouth and, wrapping my arms around Raphael, swim for the surface with all the strength left in my body. Every second counts.

Suddenly we are moving twice as quickly as my legs are pumping. Snatching another lungful of air from the mouthpiece I glance down and see one of the dolphins pushing Rafael's scuba tanks up from below. Just before we break the surface Steve, or Calypso, stops. Rafael and I bob up gently into the fresh air. The fish pen walkway is in grasping distance. I snatch at it and pull Rafael behind me, keeping his face up and out of the water. He still isn't breathing. I unfasten his weights belt, leaving it to sink to the seabed, then clamber up onto the walkway.

Even though Rafael is skinny he isn't small and his scuba tanks must weigh twenty kilos. As I haul him up out of the water onto the walkway a dolphin pushes from below.

I rip Rafael's mask off his face and roll him on his side. A little water trickles out of his mouth. Holding his nose, I lean over to breathe into his mouth. There seems to be an obstruction, I simply cannot force any air into his lungs. Unzipping his dry suit, I press my ear to his chest. I hear a heartbeat, so why isn't he breathing? I try again to give him the kiss of life. Nothing. I roll him over. A dribble more water.

Keep going, don't give up.

'Rafael, wake up. Damn you, wake up!'

I check his chest. His heartbeat is fainter than before.

'Don't you dare die on me. I promise I'll make you regret it.'

Am I doing it wrongly? He isn't dead so why isn't he breathing? Without thinking I slap his face hard then pull open his jaw to attempt the kiss of life again. Whether that does the trick or whether it is something else, I'll never know, but suddenly Rafael flinches and draws in a long high-pitched wheezing breath, then throws up.

I could never have imagined that I might feel deliriously happy at someone vomiting all over me. Life is packed with surprises.

20

'Oh, that's disgusting! They were lying there snogging and then he's just been a bad sailor all over diving suit.' Keisha burbles away, oblivious to the fact that Fred cannot hear a word she is saying. 'I mean I know it's true love and that, but do you know what I mean? She's covered in it!'

Fred snatches the binoculars from Keisha. They are still up on the hill but have moved some twenty metres away from the fire they lit with cloth, paper, and diesel fuel. The man on the boat is still standing in the cabin doorway staring up in their direction. Behind him and to his right is the big fish pen. Sam is sitting beside Rafael, holding his hand and talking to him. A couple of metres away lies the body of one of the other men. Fred takes pen and paper.

There's only one man on the surface.

Fred passes the pad to his left and picks up the binoculars. There is something wrong with Rafael's scuba equipment. Fred glances at Keisha; she hasn't even looked at his message, she is playing with a mobile phone. He takes the pen and paper and starts scribbling again.

There's no breathing thing on Rafael's scuba, it must have come off underwater. Fred shoves the paper under Keisha's nose.

Maybe they took it off to kiss, she says, her face lit by the fire.

Maybe you should shut up, he scribbles.

Keisha gives Fred the evil eye and sticks out her lower jaw, why are boys such idiots?

Where did you get that smart phone?

It was on the table, she answers.

It's not yours.

It's not yours.

What are you playing?

She refuses to show him

How long have you been doing that?

Only since we lit the fire.

That costs money. You'll be in trouble when Rafael gets the bill.

Keisha sticks out her tongue and decides not to tell Fred about the six missed calls message that were on the screen when she switched the phone on.

Fred only understands the half of it; the money it is going to cost is the least of their problems. Keisha has been connected for over ten minutes and, sixty kilometres away, the location of Rafael Santoni's smart phone is proving to be of great interest.

21

I remove his tanks and settle Rafael on his side in the recovery position at the bottom of the dinghy. He is shaken but seems otherwise OK. Strangely, he is less worried than I am and when his coughing has subsided, he explains in a weak voice something about asthmatics being taught about how the body sometimes go into shock and closes off your vocal chords and prevents you from being able to breathe.

'It is called a laryngospasm. I had it had once before, when I was eight. It scared my mum but I got over it without complications.'

'Twice before,' I correct him. 'You know with the sharks, before we found my dad? Same thing happened I think. I thought you were dead after the shark ripped your leg open. I was trying to make you draw a breath and getting nowhere then click, suddenly you were breathing again. That laryngio thingy has saved your life by preventing water from getting into your lungs.'

'I knew having asthma was lucky,' Rafael says with a wry smile.

'I'm going back down to rescue the trapped dolphins then we leave, OK?'

Rafael nods weakly. 'If I get bored and I'm not here when you come back up, I'll be surfing or waterskiing near the beach.'

'Yeah, sure.'

Before diving back down I check on my attacker, who is still lying unconscious on the walkway close by. The ropes around his wrists are tight. I tie his ankles together and secure him to one of the vertical posts of the fish pen. Using a strip of masking tape I find stuck to the side of the dinghy I make sure he won't be able to open his mouth and shout when he wakes up.

I have my torch on from the start as I descend back into the darkness. A cloud of tiny purple fish drifts in and out through the mesh of the net. Fifteen metres down Calypso is waiting for me.

'Where's Steve?' I sign.

'Gone.' The automated voice says in my headphones.

'Where?'

'Doesn't matter.'

It matters to me.

'Has Steve killed before?' I ask.

Still the smile, always the dolphin smile, but Calypso swims off in silence.

'Wait, wait,' I sign pointlessly at her retreating back. This last fish pen is so wide that I quickly lose sight of her. I follow the net round hoping to catch up. I have not seen any sign that there is anything alive within the pen, except for the cloud of tiny purple fish that are now several metres above my head. Are there any captured dolphins? Could Steve have made it up to lure us back here? Why? Calypso said that one of the dolphins called out to her. Would she lie? What would be the point? Alone underwater, I am becoming anxious and I am only partially relieved when Calypso reappears.

'Where are they?' I sign.

'Other side, further down.'

'I can't see anything in the pen.'

A burst of clicks.

'Doesn't help.' Doesn't Calypso know I cannot tap in to her echolocation?

Calypso offers her dorsal fin. In no time we are round the other side of the fish pen where, huddled together, are three dolphins. One is much smaller than the others, presumably only a few months old. One of the two adults is flinching repeatedly, left and right with its head.

'The calf is the same age as Steve was when he was captured,' Calypso tells me.

'You said there were four.'

'The sick female has died.'

As I sweep the torch beam I discover the fourth dolphin, a few metres away, a body lying on its side at the bottom of the net.

Seeing the dolphin lying there dead is horrible and I want to free the remaining dolphins as quickly as possible. I start slashing the net with my dive knife. Immediately, the three remaining dolphins show signs of extreme agitation, presumably associating me with the trauma they have already endured at the hands of the mafia. Calypso fires off a barrage of clicks and squeaks that seem to calm them down, a little. After a few seconds the baby dolphin swims towards me, curious to see what I am doing, but one of the adults rushes forwards and shepherds it away. I work as quickly as I can, not wanting to leave Rafael alone any longer than I have to. As soon the hole is wide enough Calypso swims through the gap and into the pen.

I watch her approach the dead dolphin and linger beside her, hanging in the water quite still. The hydrophone picks up a stream of whistles and clicks. I suppose it is my imagination, or the situation, but her sounds feel slower and lower than normal, like she is singing a sad song. Which is the dolphin that spoke Calypso's mother's name? Dad explained to me that the part of the brain that processes emotions is bigger in dolphins than it is in humans. For humans our attachments are often as much to things and possessions as they are to our fellow human beings, but for dolphins it is all about relationships. Although I am mad at Calypso for bringing us back into danger, who am I to demand the right to reunite my parents while denying her the right to rescue her family?

When Calypso re-emerges she is followed first by the baby then by the two adults. The last dolphin through the hole is struggling with a badly torn flipper. I shudder as I see exposed white bone high up, close to its body. How has it received such a deep cut?

'What shall we do?' I ask.

'I will swim with them to safety but we need medical help. You hurt us and now you have to heal us.'

Right, so now I am personally responsible for all the suffering in the world. There is something weird about Calypso asking for medical assistance, but then there are so many things that are weird about having direct communication with another species. She has spent nearly ten years in captivity and must have become used to relying on Dad and other people in a variety of situations.

My dive computer tells me I have air for ten minutes. To avoid getting the bends I take my time swimming back to the surface. Dad has given me graphic descriptions of what happens to a human body and has made me stare at dive tables so long I ended up wanting to feed myself to a great white shark.

I follow the net round towards the dinghy and Rafael. The cloud of tiny purple fish has reappeared and I pause in front of them, transfixed by their movement. It is like they are all tied together with invisible string. One turns, the others turn, a pulsing purple sphere in the light of my torch. Braver than before, the cloud ventures a metre beyond the safety of the net before flinching back in a violent spasm. A beat later they drift out again. What are they after? What have they found? A creeping anxiety grips me. Apart from the tiny fish, I am alone in the enveloping darkness with only the sound of my breathing for company. Without thinking, I start swimming up towards the surface, my gaze still fixed on the cloud of fish when my shoulder crunches into something hard.

22

Sven crosses the airy hall at Copenhagen airport and buys a train ticket and a sandwich. In that order. Three minutes later he is stepping onto a train leaving Denmark. Twenty minutes later he is arriving in Malmo in Sweden where he steps onto a biogas-powered bus that takes him to the Western Harbour and an extraordinary building that rises above the residential district like a strand of twisting DNA. Turning Torso. Surrounded by a pool of water and powered by renewable energy, as is the entire district it straddles, the tower is the symbol of a commitment to a new and sustainable future.

The lift disgorges him on the forty-second floor. His journey ends a few metres away, across the natural fibres of an organic carpet in front of a door bearing a plaque that reads EChO North. Two video cameras stare down at him. He raises his hand to the plaque and the door clicks open. He steps inside.

'Come in, come in. I'm Edvin. Your journey was straightforward?'

Sven nods.

'Do sit down. Coffee?'

Edvin, a slender man of medium height, with bright blue eyes, a turquoise sweater, and brown calf leather brogues, has the enviable air of someone who has no worries.

'I am sorry we have brought you so far out of your way but security is of the utmost importance in this matter, as you appreciate.

Sven's green cuboid espresso cup sits on the glass table top, appearing to float above his legs. Across the table is a second man, in his fifties, whose face he recognizes from the covers of a hundreds newspapers and websites but has never met, a man who has a personal fortune estimated to be $36 billion.

'How do you recommend that we proceed?' the man asks.

'We have to bring them in. They will not survive. Blanchard is a broken man, he and his protégés brutalized by their experiences in the Gulf and now in the Libyan War. They see enemies everywhere, not without reason, and show an alarming capacity for making new ones. Blanchard himself is now in hospital with his wife. He would wish to thank you for sorting …'

The man waves Sven's thanks aside.

'Are you certain that this inter-species communication narrative is for real?'

'I have witnessed one side of the story, seen the complexity of the sign language employed by Blanchard in his communications with the dolphins, film of which I believe you have also …'

'Yes.'

'The whole family is fluent in sign language, the result of the profound deafness of Blanchard's son, so it can be assumed that the daughter is now communicating …'

'And the dolphins themselves have modified their vocalisations to enable a software system to be developed that can translate their communication in English?'

'That's it.'

'Remarkable.'

'Blanchard is a genius. Flawed but …'

'They usually are. Where are they?'

'I don't know,' Sven shakes his head. 'They left Elba, the daughter, the Italian boy and two children, apparently, before two o'clock this afternoon. After the explosion. The whereabouts of the two dolphins is unknown. But when they make contact we have to act.'

'Understood. The question is how to act covertly. I do not want to be seen to thwart the endeavours of national armies and or governments, nor do I particularly relish a head on confrontation with organized crime or the private defence sector. I am also painfully aware of what happened on that Eurostar train to Paris three weeks ago. We lost two good people.'

'There are alternatives,' Sven says quietly.

23

Dislodged by the shifting currents, the dead man's face drops down in front of my own, bulging eyes staring blindly, the head bobbing up and down gently in the water. Rafael's attacker has become tangled in the net and his face, now drained of blood, is ghostly white. A tiny purple fish swims out of the open mouth; that's what has brought them out into the open water.

If the small fish has found him it is only a matter of time before other creatures appear. Creatures with huge jaws and teeth.

Calm down Sam.

With the net at my back I swim straight up, following my bubbles.. The sea is such a mixture of conflicting emotions. I love it and am in wonder of it, particularly while I am busy doing something. On the other hand, underwater I feel trapped and encased in the infinite gloom, pushed back and forth by invisible currents.

Up on the surface, one fear is replaced by another; pond skater syndrome, the sense of being little more than a speck floating on a world of danger you cannot see into.

I spit out the mouthpiece and follow the perimeter of fish pen towards the dinghy. To cheer me up, it has started to rain.

Pulling myself up, I flop into the dinghy beside Rafael, and remove my scuba tanks.

His eyes open. 'What took you so long?'

'The calf is so beautiful, Rafael. I wish we could kill the bastards who are doing this. One of the other dolphins died and another has a really nasty injury to its flipper.'

'I hope Calypso and Steve appreciate what you just did. It's creepy down there alone. Can we go now?'

As he speaks, I have an idea. 'You were worried about fuel before we set off. There's no way we can reach France now with what we have, is there? Let's take some from this ship.'

'It won't be hanging around in drums,' Rafael says. 'And how we will get it to the boat?'

'We've got a dinghy.'

I pick up the oars and drop them into the oarlocks. Beside me, Rafael pushes himself up into a sitting position.

I shake my head. 'I'll do it. The recently dead should avoid serious exercise.'

He grimaces.

'Even arching your eyebrows is not recommended.'

'I wasn't dead. Is smiling OK?'

'Whatever.' I relent a little. 'Have you seen an umbrella? I am getting seriously wet.'

Untying the rope that secures the dinghy to the fish pen, I push off, cursing the genius who decided that rowers must always travel backwards.

The mafia ship is at least thirty metres long. A light is on in one of the aft portholes, close to the waterline. I try to remember if it was on earlier. From the water, it is hard to see the safest point to try to scale the ship. Closing my eyes for a second, I remind myself of what we saw from the hill. Towards the stern is an A-frame above the deck to carry the thick cable that attaches to the nets when they are being dragged. I remember the portable ladder that hangs over the side but that is on the other side of the ship, the same side as the open door through which we saw the legs of the person sitting in the cabin.

The stern seems the best bet. The hull is lower at that point and a mess of fishing nets and ropes offer cover as I climb aboard, scrambling up without much difficulty; being tall is working to my advantage. The deck slopes upward and, having told Rafael to give me ten minutes, I crawl forwards then crouch behind the nets to study the ship's layout.

Rafael is right about there being no jerry cans of fuel sitting about on deck, but that isn't all I am after. There are three levels of accommodation, the lowest of which is straight ahead, a few steps down. Towards the front of the boat is a second tier, and right at the top and furthest away from me is the pilothouse. Aside from the light coming from the porthole, which Rafael thinks is in the ship's engine room, the ship is in darkness. A good sign.

Rigging clicks in the breeze. Black rain falls hard, bouncing and splashing off every surface. I wrinkle my nose, there is a strong smell of diesel fumes and ripe fish. Before continuing, I grab a small tarpaulin and drop it down to Rafael in the dinghy. No point in him freezing to death.

I skirt the nets, down the steps and, keeping below the windows, inch toward the door on the lowest level. Maybe there have only been two people on board, the men who had attacked us, but a ship this size must accommodate fifteen people or more. No more surprises.

I gently turn the door handle and pull. The rusty hinges groan. Two choices: slow or quick. I choose quick to get it over with, and yank the door open, hoping that if there is anyone to hear the sound they will mistake it for the groaning of the ship. A tatty carpet muffles my footsteps as I slip inside, glad to get the rain off my back. I leave the door open behind me, in case I need a rapid escape.

A faint motor sound whirs in the background. A fridge or a freezer? The room is large with windows on both sides of the ship and, in the half light, I see various posters on the walls. I flick my torch on for a second. A football team, a couple of girls posing in bikinis, some official looking notices. Beside the dartboard, into which are buried a fistful of darts, is a large photo of a priest dressed in white. The Pope? Tired and tatty chairs hug the walls, maybe ten in all, like in a doctor's waiting room. A couple of tables carry ashtrays and packs of playing cards. The room stinks of stale cigarette smoke.

I step through a doorway that leads toward the front of the ship. The corridor is so dark that I am obliged to switch on my torch, shielding the beam with my hand so only the thinnest slither of light escapes.

The nameplate on the first door on the left reads Capitano. Opposite is a second door: Medico. The door opens easily and I cross the threshold. As I do so, another doors open further down the corridor.

I am not alone.

24

'What are they doing?'

Fred shrugs. He puts the binoculars down beside him and rummages for the notepad tucked in his shirt.

Rafael is sitting in the small boat and Sam has disappeared on the ship, he scribbles on a dry patch of paper. As soon as Keisha has finished reading, he stuffs the pad away, out of the rain.

'Yer sister's a tatty head. Going on that boat is stupid. She's soft as candy-floss that one.'

The fire is dying down, only the big tree still burns, the rain has quenched everything else. Soaked to the skin, the two children are shivering. Though neither has said anything, they are each realising how close they are to being alone.

'Shall we light another fire?'

Fred shakes his head. In all the time they have been watching the ship they have seen just three men, the two who went over to the fish pen and the person who until a few moments ago has been sitting in the pilot's cabin.

Keisha, peering through the binoculars, nudges Fred's shoulder, 'He's not dead, is he?'

Fred takes the binoculars back. Only Rafael's head is visible, the rest of him hidden beneath the large dark sheet. He is lying against the side of the dinghy, eyes closed. Fred begins to panic, adjusting the focus on the binoculars, hoping to see that Rafael is still breathing. He is too far away.

More shaking of his shoulder. 'I'm scared.'

Me too, Fred scribbles. Let's go back.

The two children pick themselves up and make their way through the bushes. They sprint past the deserted ruins, fearful of its dark shadows, and on towards the cove. In the pouring rain, the path down to the cove is even more dangerous than before. Taking their time, they test each and every loose rock before putting their weight on it, and hide beneath every overhang until their desire to be warm and dry overwhelms their fear of falling.

Time and again one or other of them stumbles, their feet landing awkwardly or catching against an exposed root. Halfway down, Fred's left shoe slips from under him and he crumples, banging his shoulder heavily as he falls. Keisha screams, snatching the straps of his rucksack and pulling with all her strength. But it is not enough. The pair slide ever more quickly towards the drop, accompanied by dislodged stones that clatter and crash downwards onto the shingle some ten metres below. Fred throws himself onto his side, breaking his fingernails as he claws desperately at the dirt, but his forward momentum is too strong. His feet dangle over the edge in open space.

Then, just as he feels his weight pulling him over the brink, he stops moving. Keisha, still clinging to his rucksack with one hand, has managed to grab a bush that is holding firm. Slowly the two children wriggle back from the edge. They lie in the dirt, catching their breaths. A little further and they will be safe.

They pick themselves up and recommence their descent. A low rumbling sound stops Keisha in her tracks. As the sound grows it becomes more rhythmic, like the sound washing machines make sometimes when they are spinning washing. Fred, who hears nothing, is still climbing down. Keisha scrambles after him. They reach the shingle as the beating sound grows dramatically and a helicopter appears overhead, its searchlight sweeping across the cove and lighting up the boat. Keisha leaps up and down, waving her hands above her head.

'Oh yeah, we're being rescued! Over here,' she shouts. 'Amazing, we're all gonna ride in a helicopter. Wait till the star struck lovers see this!'

Fred looks at the helicopter then back at Keisha's broad grin. Her excitement is infectious and he smiles back, but inside he isn't so sure that things are about to get better.

25

I crouch in the darkness behind the desk. The footsteps approach slowly, pausing from time to time as doors are opened and closed. There are two portholes behind me, too small for anyone to climb through other than a small child. Trapped, I quietly release my knife from its sheath and try to imagine myself leaping up and seizing the initiative.

Like it is easy to kill someone, Sam. Get real.

The footsteps stop once more, close enough for me to hear fingers drumming quietly on the open door. I hold my breath until my head is spinning from lack of oxygen. The feet move away.

'Paolo?' The words echo in the large room at the end of the corridor. 'Paolo?

I take a breath. Who is Paolo? I stand up carefully, poised to run as soon as I hear the creaking hinge of the exterior door.

A torch shines straight into my eyes, blinding me.

'Chi sei?'

I raise a hand to cover my eyes.

'Cada la lama.' The voice is soft and rasping. 'I said drop the knife.'

I hear a click. I drop the knife.

'Good.'

A second click. The room is bathed in light from the fluorescent tube on the ceiling. In front of me is a wiry old man in a t-shirt, blue overalls, a thick white moustache, and a drinker's nose covered in thread-like veins. His thick chaotic eyebrows leave his eyes in deep shadow. He holds a gun. I can smell the alcohol on his breath from across the room.

'I was looking for medicine. There's been an accident and I …'

'Sit down, my friend.' The old man uses the barrel of his gun to point where I should sit, on the floor.

I do as I am told.

'Tell me, where are my companions?'

'I don't know. We have just …'

‘Stop. I will ask you once more and this time I suggest that you think before you open your mouth.’ He points his pistol at my chest.

‘They attacked us …’

‘Us?’

‘Rafael and I. At the fish pen where you were keeping dolphins.’

‘This Rafael, he is also a child?’

‘I am sixteen.’ Give or take a couple of hours.

‘You are a child.’

Yeah, whatever, I think to myself, and you’re a miserable old drunk; but you don’t say that to a man holding a gun. ‘They attacked us, we defended ourselves,’ I volunteer instead. ‘The one who attacked me is unconscious and tied up. The other man is dead. He drowned.’

The old man says nothing for a moment then his face breaks into a grim smile. ‘Idiots, the pair of them. So now you tell me why you are here. Were you here last night?’

I ignore the second question.

‘We came to rescue the dolphins. You have no right to …’

‘A couple of children come to steal half a million euros.’

I must look surprised.

‘Half a million. And last night our tuna nets were cut. Another million euros, maybe more. I hope you come from a rich family. The ransom will be very large.’

‘When all the fish have been killed and the sea is dead, how will your children live?’ I ask. ‘What will they eat? What jobs will they have?’

‘And if I stop hunting, do you think no-one will take my place? I am nothing. You and I cannot save the world. There are five hundred smuggling rings catching blue fin tuna in the Mediterranean to sell to the Japanese. The same for the dolphins. If we do not catch wild dolphins to sell to the theme parks do you think the theme parks will close? I speak good English, yes?’

I nod.

‘I have travelled everywhere. Everywhere is just like here, my young friend.’

‘One dolphin is only a baby.’

‘They are more valuable. You want to know why we capture dolphins?

‘No, not really.’

'I was once a dreamer like you. Before I grew this white moustache. I watched my first child die because I had no work. I called him Vittorio, like me. But he was a fool, he refused to eat my fine principles or my righteous anger or my noble courage and so he starved to death. And so my wife left, and I grew up. Now we fill our fish pens with dolphins and tuna and my village has forgotten hunger. You too will grow up. Come,' he says, waving the gun. 'I have a room below deck where we will keep you until someone pays back the money you have cost us. I hope you like the smell of fish.'

The old man stands away from the desk, still facing me as I start to climb to my feet. Another voice, a new voice, says something in Italian. I realise again how badly I have miscalculated everything.

But I am not the only one thinking this. The old man looks as surprised as I am. He is still turning when a dark object flashes behind his head, followed by a sickening crunch. The old man's face registers confusion as he sinks slowly to his knees, staring straight at me. Behind him stands Rafael clutching an iron bar. For what seem like minutes the man is kneeling in front of me then, finally, he slumps forward, landing face down on the floor.

Rafael glances at his watch then up at me. 'Happy birthday.'

'What took you so long?'

Rafael smiles. 'I thought you were looking for diesel.'

'That and some medical kit to fix a broken flipper, and all the evidence we can find on what the Mafia are doing.'

We take an envelope from a drawer and stuff it with bandages, painkillers, antiseptics, antibiotics, scissors and scalpels. I collect my knife off the floor, and the old man's gun and, stepping over the body, we go out into the corridor. In the Capitano's cabin Rafael finds the ship's log book.

'The other boats have gone towards Corsica, according to this, to capture more dolphins. Listen to this, the ship is called Serena. Can you believe it? A mafia ship called peaceful.'

'Where? Where exactly are they going?'

'West,' Rafael quotes from the log, translating into English for my benefit.. 'A superpod of sixty dolphins according to someone called Mario.'

'OK, let's take the log book. Maybe there are charts in the pilot's cabin. I'll go. If I'm not back in …'

'Don't start that again,' Rafael says. 'This time we go together.'

26

Stairs at the end of the corridor lead straight up two flights. I run and in seconds I am in the pilot's cabin. Rafael, who has reluctantly agreed to walk, joins me a short while later, carrying the medical supplies we have taken. He is out of breath and looks unwell. In spite of the door to the outside being open, there is an acrid smell of wine, cigarettes, stale sweat and garlic in the air. The rain hammers on the roof.

'Sit down. Don't be a hero, Rafa.' I practically have to shout above the noise. Since when have I started calling him Rafa?

'They may have printed a chart. You can now download and print when you need it. The latest technology.'

These guys don't do latest technology. There is no printer, but I do find a stack of charts in a cupboard and, more importantly, I find the waste paper bin. I tip the contents onto the table, having first pushed aside four empty bottles of wine and a large stinking ashtray. Among the rubbish, olive stones, empty cigarette packets, lotto tickets, paper tissues, and half-eaten sandwiches, are two crumpled maps.

We spread out the first map, a very detailed nautical chart of the waters around Montecristo Island, showing water depths, obstructions, and tide differences.

'Look, they have marked the locations of the fish pens.' Rafael says, over my shoulder. 'This is evidence.'

I have no idea yet who we are going to present evidence to, but I roll up the chart and hand it to him.

If you threw an ice cream at a wall the resulting splat would look pretty much like the island in the middle of the second chart.

'Where is it?'

'The co-ordinates are not very different to the ones for Montecristo so it cannot be very far.'

'But it's in French.' I point at various descriptions on the map.

'What's your problem?'

‘France is two or three hundred kilometres north.’

‘Corsica is only fifty kilometres west. And Corsica is part of France.’

‘They’ve gone to France to steal dolphins?’

‘How would I know?’ Rafael asks nonplussed.

‘We have to stop them.’

‘What? A recently dead youth, a sixteen year old girl, and two dolphins? We’re going to stop a major mafia operation?’

‘You forgot to mention Fred and Keisha. Was that an oversight or was it deliberate?’

‘Ha ha,’ he laughs sarcastically. ‘I thought we were sticking with your Dad’s plan,’ Rafael reminds me as we roll up the chart. ‘We’ll take this with us,’ he adds, unplugging the satellite communication system, ‘in case your friend downstairs wakes up.’

We go back down. The old man is still in the medical room. He has rolled over onto his side and is snoring, an ugly patch of blood on the floor beneath his head. Back in the large room, I hesitate on the threshold.

‘Come on, it’s only rain and we’re wearing dry suits.’

Yeah, right, what am I worrying about?

I partially unzip my dry suit and squeeze the charts in between the rubber and my t-shirt, then zip back up.

We make our way aft towards the dinghy, treading carefully as we negotiate the slippery sloping deck.

‘Oops!’ Rafael says, dropping the satellite communications rack into the sea. ‘I’m so clumsy. Do you still want to look for fuel? And something to put it in?’

‘Could we reach Corsica?’

He nods.

‘Let’s just go.’

We climb into the dinghy. Thirty metres away, the man I bound and gagged earlier is wide wake and wriggling but the knots are holding. By the time he is found we will be far away.

A dorsal fin pops up close by; Calypso has found us. She treats us to a barrage of clicks and whistles. I grab my scuba kit and pull the iPad out of its waterproof sleeve, but the battery is dead. Without the iPad neither Rafael nor I can understand what she is telling us. Rafael points the torch beam towards me while I explain to Calypso what has happened. That done I pick up the oars to row us back to the cove. Immediately Calypso blocks our path. More clicks and whistles.

'She wants us to stay here,' Rafael suggests. 'Maybe something has happened to the baby dolphin.'

'I don't care,' I retort, signing at the same time as speaking. 'It's pouring. We're both tired, we have to get back.'

Calypso is staring at the pair of us and repeating the same two words over and over. I understand them but I do not translate them for Rafael.

Danger, boat, boat, danger.

Whatever danger there is in the cove it cannot be worse than the danger we face if we stay where we are.

'OK Calypso, I understand, but you have to let us pass. If we stay here we will die.'

She is still smiling but clearly angry when she turns away and sinks beneath the waves.

It takes nearly half an hour to row the kilometre back to the cove. I refuse to allow Rafael to do any of the rowing, he has to sit and watch as I slowly run out of steam. Fortunately for us the tide is out, which isn't saying much in this part of the Mediterranean where the difference between high tide and low tide is only forty centimetres, but it is enough to reveal some of the razor sharp, barnacle covered rocks at the entrance to the cove. I row between them and hope we can avoid the others.

The boat is where we left it. There is no sign of anything being amiss so why is Calypso warning us to stay away? It doesn't make sense.

Everything is in darkness, the children must have given up and gone to sleep, which is all I want to do. I check my dive computer, time 00:43, temperature twelve degrees, depth zero metres. Happy Birthday, Sam.

Rafael is first up the portable ladder.

'Hey, stay there, I'm passing the kit up to you. Rafa, Rafael!' No answer. Why am I not surprised? He has just waltzed off. 'Yay, OK, I'll do everything by myself, thanks,' I call up. Muttering under my breath, I tie the dinghy to the ladder, sling a set of dive tanks over my shoulder and, exhausted, start to climb. Only when I reach the height of the deck do I see what has happened.

27

On the beach, previously hidden behind the boat, is a helicopter. On the deck of La Vita Nuova is a slim woman in a trouser suit holding a gun. It is unreal, like being in an old black and white film.

'Do you have to point that?' I ask.

Rafael is lying on his front in front of her.

'Put everything down very slowly then lie down next to pretty boy.'

'Pretty boy?'

'Just do it and no-one will get hurt.'

'Where are my brother and the girl?' I ask as I swing the scuba tanks off my shoulder and place them gently on the deck.

Idiot, Sam. Why did you tell her about the other two?

I sit down on the deck, staring up at her. The woman keeps glancing over my shoulder as if expecting someone else. Finally, she tosses a pair of handcuffs at me.

'One side for you, one side for him.'

'What have we done?' I ask.

'Just do it.'

'What have we done?'

In one movement the woman swings the gun up to the left, fires a shot, and brings the gun back to point at my chest. The bullet ricochets off the rocks behind me.

Having closed a cuff on my left hand I inch sideways on my backside until I am next to Rafael. I lie on my back and click the other cuff around his wrist.

Sidestepping us, the woman crosses the boat. In another practised and rapid movement she swings her gun to point down into the dinghy.

'There's only us,' I say.

'Get up.'

Only as we make to stand up do I realise my mistake. I have cuffed Rafael's left wrist because he is lying face down. We are now facing in opposite directions.

'Get inside.'

It isn't easy walking with someone stuck to your back, in fact it's ridiculously difficult. We enter the cabin. The woman switches on the lights.

'Sit.'

We sit at the table, me facing the table, Rafael facing backward. I can't help myself, a combination of being really tired and stressed and fed up, that and the fact that Fred and Keisha are sitting in the corner, staring wide-eyed at us like we are completely insane. I start giggling.

'Is something amusing?' the woman asks, her voice soft and calm.

'Well, it's just that …' I start.

'Is this amusing?' She smashes the butt of her pistol into my shoulder blade. I cry out as the pain explodes across my back.

She kicks one of the steel table legs to check the table is screwed securely to the floor then produces a second set of handcuffs, clicks one cuff round Rafael's right wrist and the other round a table leg, then unlocks the cuff that ties Rafael to me.

'Turn round and sit there and close the other cuff round the same table leg.'

By the time I have finished, we are sitting at right angles to each other, Rafael shackled to the table leg with his right hand and me to the same table leg with my left hand.

The woman has dark brown eyes, a thin hooked nose, like a hawk's beak, and blond streaks in her shoulder length hair. There is something ugly or cruel about her mouth, which seems too small for her face.

'Where is your father?'

'My father is dead,' Rafael says. 'The military killed him.'

'You.'

I shrug.

'And the dolphins?'

I shrug again.

The woman stares at me the way tigers stare at the public in a zoo; that dispassionate look that is only ever a moment from extreme violence.

'For me this is just a job,'

‘You’re not the first person to point a gun at me tonight. To be honest, I’ve had enough. Welcome to my birthday. If you want to shoot a bunch of children then just get on and do it.’

Her eyes stay fixed on mine.

‘I hope you get paid well for what you do,’ I add. ‘I hope it’s worth it.’

‘Your father has stolen something very expensive and my job is to retrieve the items for their owners.’

‘What has he stolen?’

‘Highly trained dolphins that belong to the military.’

‘Which army?’

‘I am not at liberty …’

‘Neither were the dolphins.’

‘I am not having a discussion with you.’

‘No, you’re like the others; following orders, destroying the world.’

‘They’re super dolphins, these ones. They can talk,’ says a small voice behind me. ‘You’re not allowed to touch them.’

‘Keisha, mind your own business’ I say.

‘Sam told me that they couldn’t talk, right? But I’ve got eyes, me. They’ve got a computer and it turns dolphin talk into English and …’

‘Shut … up,’ I say.

Fred catches my eye and starts signing frantically. Are we all going to die? Are the dolphins OK? What happened to the men on the ship?

‘Fred said it was my fault the helicopter came, but I didn’t know, did I?’

A phone starts ringing.

‘Stop,’ the woman shouts.

We stop. She pulls the phone out of her pocket, and checks the identity of the caller.

‘Nobody move,’ she says, pulling open the cabin door and stepping outside.

28

'I trust the expense of the helicopter has not been wasted,' Tenebris says.

He knows already. She should have expected that. Pressing the phone closer to her ear, Vikki Gutner stands far enough away from the cabin window to be out of earshot while still keeping an eye on the children inside.

'I have located the boat.'

'Good. And the occupants?'

'The daughter, the Santoni boy, and two young children.'

The young boy has his face glued to the window, staring at her.

'Michel Blanchard and the assets?'

'The interrogation is about to start, the Blanchard girl and Santoni arrived only a few minutes ago.'

'Do not waste time. When you are finished, kill them all and sink the boat. I will send a team to track the dolphins.'

'They are children.'

'Your point being?'

'I have question regarding the dolphins,' Gutner says, changing tack.

Tenebris remains silent.

'What is special about them?' she asks.

'I suggest you spend the little time you have on matters that concern you.'

29

'But you would rather see them destroyed than allowed to escape? Are you sure that's what she said?' I sign for Fred and speak at the same time for the other two.

'She asked what is special about the dolphins, then she asked if they should be destroyed rather than being allowed to escape,' Fred signs back.

'He can read her mouth through the windows?' Keisha says in awe.

'What have windows got to do with anything?' Rafael says.

'Has she said who she is talking to?' I sign and speak.

'Michel Blanchard is not here. When I arrived there were only the two small children. One has learning difficulties and the other cannot be more than ten years old.' Fred continues reading the woman's lips as she speaks. Only his face is visible to her outside in the rain, she cannot see his hands talking, or mine. 'So I'm stupid, according to her,' Fred adds.

'Everything is under control, I do not need reinforcements,' Fred lip reads and signs.

The woman's eyes narrow a fraction. I wish I could hear the voice in her ear.

'Understood … Yes.' Fred turns towards us 'She has finished the call.'

I look through the window. The woman is standing in the rain, phone pressed to her ear, staring out towards the open sea. Who does she work for? How much danger are we in?

'Switch it off and take the battery out,' Rafael says. 'Now.'

Across the cabin Keisha, who appears to have decided that playing with Rafael's smart phone is more interesting than listening to the rest of us, suddenly looks up, eyes blazing. 'Hey! Grab a thinking doughnut and get yer teeth round this,' she announces.

'Just switch my phone off. And what does that even mean? A what doughnut?'

‘It’s something my dad says when …’ Keisha starts then pauses, visibly angry that the present tense is now a traitor in her mouth. Fists clenched, she somehow manages to control one set of emotions and return to the other. ‘Listen, we pour oil on the floor then, when that tatty head comes back in, she slides across, knocks herself out and we …’

‘You watch too many cartoons,’ I say. Then I remember something. ‘But we could do this.’

‘Oh, what!’ says Keisha, beaming from ear to ear.

30

Gutner watches the waves breaking beyond the cove. Past midnight; she has less than twelve hours before Tenebris sets the dogs after her. In a way she looks forward to it. In the context of a dangerous operation no-one will reproach her a couple of casualties. But she will have to prepare thoroughly, there will be no second chance. Play her cards right and she can complete her mission, kill her principal rivals and be back in Sicily by midnight.

But gaining respect from Tenebris will not be enough, she will need to have something he wants, a bargaining chip to secure her own future.

Gutner turns back to the window. An argument is taking place, the Blanchard girl is waving her finger at the younger children. What did the young girl say? Are the dolphins simply trained military assets or is there another dimension to everything? What is Tenebris hiding?

A liquid sound catches her ear. A dorsal fin has just broken the water some fifteen metres from the boat. She watches it cutting a track through the dark waters then disappear beneath the surface. She pulls out her pistol; is this one of the animals she is tasked with capturing or killing?

Persuading the two older children to work with her is key; there is no point in capturing or killing one dolphin if, in doing so, she drives the other one away. The job will only be complete when both dolphins, the Blanchard girl and her father, and Rafael Santoni are no longer in circulation. She still has to locate Michel Blanchard. Just a few days ago Michel, his daughter and the Santoni boy were together. What has happened?

She has a couple of other calls to make; the children aren't going anywhere.

31

Calypso meanders back and forth in the waters of the cove, her belly occasionally rubbing against the small stones that rock gently in the current. She is at a complete loss as to what she should do next. For as long as she can remember Michel has been there, to guide her, work with her, listen to her. They have faced everything together and though fragments of memories of her life prior to her capture remain, Michel's absence leaves a huge aching void.

At the start he was her tormentor, training her to do things she had no interest in doing, preventing her from escaping, organising her every moment with pointless tests. Only gradually, as she saw him defend her from other humans, had she begun to realise that he was not like the others. He protected her, insisted that she be given space and time off. Once, when a harness was fitted that cut into her ribs, Michel pushed the other humans away and redid the straps, and he had taken a beating more than once while defending the dolphins from the humans who carried weapons. Eventually she understood that just as she was, he was a prisoner.

On their first missions, to detect mines in the hot shallow sea, she had thought many times of escape but two things held her back, her growing friendship with Michel, and her determination to protect Steve no matter what.

Sometimes it seems to Calypso that Steve isn't a dolphin at all. With no memory of a life before his capture he feels no joy in the sea, no sense of being at one with the waves, and little kinship with other dolphins. He can barely communicate with wild members of his species. For Steve, hunting means looking for mines, not looking for food. When he is hungry he expects to be fed. When he is ill he expects to be treated. He is a mess. She knows it is not his fault, he was only a baby when he was captured, but that doesn't change the fact that Steve is a danger to himself and to everyone around him.

She knows things that she has never told anyone else, dolphin or human. Steve vanished immediately after killing Rafael's attacker. Calypso knows that Steve will be feeling vulnerable, angry and alone. She feels the same way. Beyond the cove are the dolphins they have rescued from the net, waiting for her to return to help them, and on the boat are Sam and Rafael and the calves. Calypso knows that Michel would want her to protect them, but how?

She surfaces again in the dark waters of the cove, parting the waters so gently that there is barely a ripple. The woman is still on deck, talking into the phone. Calypso understands what telephones do; Michel showed her a long time ago. Who is the woman? Is she a friend or an enemy?

Passing the boat, Calypso sees the helicopter and understands that this is how the woman arrived. Both Calypso and Steve have been carried in helicopters hundreds of times as the soldiers move them from conflict zone to conflict zone. Is the woman a soldier?

Burdened with unanswered and unanswerable questions, Calypso re-submerges and swims out of the cove.

32

Vikki Gutner throws open the cabin door, gun in hand, and steps out of the rain. She isn't in the habit of underestimating people but in a split second she realises that she has completely misread the situation. Her foot slips away from under her, causing her to throw her body to the side in a desperate attempt to regain her balance. At the same time she realises that neither of the two older children is still seated at the table. But since they are both handcuffed to the table that cannot be possible.

Still trying to make sense of this, while sliding across the floor, when something hard and very heavy smashes against her hip. Her body crumples awkwardly, a searing pain surging in her thigh. While her body has reached the floor her head has not yet stopped moving. She glimpses two young children's faces peering through the door at the end of the cabin then her face hits one of the legs of the table and the world fades to black.

33

'How did you know?' Rafael asks.

I blush. 'It's a gift, like x-ray vision or extra sensory perception, or being able to eat a kilo of chocolate in one go without throwing up. I just look at a table and I can tell if the top is properly screwed in from underneath.'

'Really?'

'Yes, Keisha, really. Hello? Hasn't irony reached Liverpool yet?'

'Course it has, we invented it, know what I mean?'

I turn back towards Rafael. 'I was cleaning up the cabin last week sometime, while you and Dad were fishing, on my hands and knees under the table then I forgot and stood up.'

'I knew that, by the way,' Keisha cuts in. 'And anyway, it's called sarcasm not irony.'

I ignore her. 'I meant to tell Dad, in case there was a storm or something.'

'Hey, don't forget genius number two,' Keisha pipes up. 'and my brilliant oil on the floor thang. Oh yeah.'

I relent and ruffle her hair. 'You did all right, kid.'

Keisha celebrates by holding both her thumbs up and showing them to each of us in turn. Rafael claps politely. Keisha bows.

'What do we do with her?' Fred signs and points at the unconscious woman on the floor.

'We find out who she is,' I sign and say, squatting down beside her and rummaging in her pockets.

'That's stealing.'

'Get a life, Keisha.'

I retrieve the keys to the handcuffs, remembering the pocket from which she took them. Rafael and I remove our cuffs and use both pairs to fasten the woman's wrists together.

Also in her pockets are her mobile phone, a beautiful leather wallet and a bunch of keys. And that is it. The Banca D'Italia credit card in her wallet reads Vikki Gutner.

‘See what you can learn from that then toss it in the sea.’ I pass the phone to Rafael.

In the background Fred is waving something. I leap up and take it from him before someone is injured. ‘Where’s the safety catch on a pistol, Rafael?’

‘I don’t know about guns.’

‘Really? You knew all about that gun in the rucksack that Sven gave you in Brussels the day we met.

‘Because I read the instructions. All I know is that if it is a Glock then it doesn’t have a safety catch.’

I give him an is-that-meant-to-be-helpful? look.

‘It was in a movie.’

‘How do I know if it is a Glock?’

No answer. I shove Gutner’s gun in the drawer beside the wheel.

‘Nobody open it. You two need to try to get some sleep. Rafael and I are going to take the woman back to her helicopter then we can leave.’

Fred and Keisha don’t protest; we are all dog-tired.

I take her feet, Rafael her shoulders, and we half-drag, half-carry the woman out of the cabin. There is no easy way of getting her off the boat. We lift her and, shivering in the rain, I balance her on the gunwale while Rafael climbs down into the dinghy. I do my best to lower her carefully towards Rafael, but she is too heavy and I am too cold. With her feet a metre above the dinghy I let go and she falls in a heap, almost tipping the dinghy over. Climbing down and joining them, I row the boat ashore.

I cannot lift the woman into the helicopter by myself and there is no way I will let Rafael help. He has to rest, the memory of him lying on the fish pen walkway not breathing less than two hours ago is still too fresh. We roll her between the landing skids underneath the fuselage, out of the rain, which is more than she deserves. She is on her side, still unconscious, still handcuffed. I take her money and put the wallet back in her pocket.

There is a briefcase on one of the three seats. We pull open the doors and lean in from opposite sides of the helicopter.

‘This is smaller than my mum’s Smart car,’ I say, taking the briefcase, opening it, and pulling out a bunch of papers.

‘But it flies, which makes it one hundred per cent more cool.’

‘You haven’t seen my mum’s car.’ Every document in Italian I pass across the cabin to Rafael, which leaves me with one report written in English and an iPad.

‘Look at this, our names, the ports we’ve stopped at, stuff about the boat …’

‘Here, listen. Name: Vikki Gutner. Company: 3-TEC. Address: Palermo, Sicily. Model: Hiller UH12B. Hire terms: 3 days.’

Rafael frowns. ‘3-TEC? We heard that name before somewhere.’

‘Gutner is a German name. Same as on the credit card.’

‘So what?’

‘We’ll take this stuff with us. Are helicopters really tricky to fly?’ I ask, looking at all the dials and buttons.

‘Not so difficult.’

‘Oh, you’re a pilot as well?’

‘They’re just a bigger version of a model helicopter.’

Before I can present a witty put down my feet are yanked away from under me and I fall back heavily on the shingle, my ankles held in a vice-like grip.

34

I howl as Gutner's fingernails tear into my flesh. Her wrists still handcuffed together, she hauls me under the helicopter. I kick out but she is too strong for me. Too late I understand what she is doing. Having braced herself against one of the vertical bars of the landing skids, she drags me rapidly towards her then, in one rapid and seamless movement, releases my ankles, swings her good leg round and kicks me violently towards one of the other vertical bars. The cold metal slams me in the neck, crushing my already fragile windpipe with such force that I can no longer breathe. My arms flail about trying to reach her, to force her to relinquish the pressure, but my fingers find only fresh air.

Dizzy, dimly thinking that someone or something should be helping me, I hear her roar from her exertions and suddenly none of it matters anymore; sound and vision flies into distant irrelevance, and a black tunnel opens up and swallows me whole.

When I awake, I am coughing so hard I expect to see bits of my lungs flying out of my mouth. Water is pouring into my face and I have the weirdest feeling that I am out of control and floating in space.

'Don't say anything,' a familiar voice says.

I open my eyes. Rafael is leaning over me. 'When you're ready I will help you climb into the boat.'

My head rolls to the side. We are in the dinghy; he must have carried me.

'Where is she?' I say, tensing up.

'She's not a problem anymore.'

'You killed her?' In panic, I try to sit up, there is too much death. Where are Fred and Keisha?

Rafael gently pushes me back. 'Relax. I didn't kill anyone. She will have a headache, that's all. I used the handcuffs to tie her to the skid bar. As soon as you are OK we have to get away. We can't still be here when they come to rescue her.'

My neck is throbbing. Swallowing is all but impossible. Rafael offers me his hand and pulls me into a sitting position. The effort leaves him coughing. We are, as my Mum would say, a right pair. Although the rain has slowed, I am shivering uncontrollably.

To our left three dorsal fins break the surface of the cove.

'Calypso has been asking about you.'

'How long was I …'

'About fifteen minutes. She pulled the dinghy over to the boat.'

Calypso's head appears out of the water close to the dinghy.

'Hi Calypso,' I sign. 'Thank you.'

A torrent of clicks and squeaks follows, of which I only understand the first word: Sam.

'Is Steve back?' I ask.

'No.'

'Is she going to die from losing all that blood?' Keisha is leaning over the side of the boat, pointing a torch down at us .

'Don't be stupid,' Rafael says. 'It's not as bad as it looks.'

'How bad does it look?' I ask.

'It's a cut. I'll get you some painkillers.'

I run a hand through my hair. The sight of blood galvanises me. Grabbing the portable ladder, I drag myself up onto my feet. Rafael reaches out to help me but I brush him away.

'Where's Fred?' I ask once I have made it up the ladder and joined Keisha on deck.

'Follow the noise. It's like the jets landing at John Lennon Airport.'

She has a point. For someone who hardly makes a sound when awake, Fred makes up for it with his snoring while he sleeps.

Rafael hurries to the cabin and re-emerges with a hydrophone, the laptop, a large tube of antiseptic cream, and a strip of codeine tablets.

I think I'll have a wash first,' I say, swallowing a couple of pills and taking the cream from him. 'You can help me, Keisha.'

'Do we have to shave all the hair off your head?'

''Yeah, and yours too, so you don't catch anything off me.'

She turns and scarpers.

'Joke,' I shout after her.

'I knew that,' she shouts back but doesn't reappear.

A few minutes later, wearing a warm jumper and anorak, and with my hair wrapped in a towel, I sit on a crate at the back of the boat to talk with Calypso.

'We have another long journey,' I sign, 'so we leave straightaway.'

'No,' the laptop screen reads.

'Look, I understand, we're all tired, Calypso, but once we have put twenty kilometres between us and these fish pens we can stop and chat …'

'No.'

'Just find Steve and tell him we are going. If he doesn't come now, he will have to catch us up.'

'It is not Steve I am worried about. There's the calf, and the other dolphins. They need time to …'

'Sorry, Calypso. You're don't understand.'

'No, you don't understand.' Calypso leaps out of the water and crashes down, smashing her flukes hard on the surface, spraying the boat and me with water. 'You are only a child.' She disappears from view. 'Leave us now, this is over.'

Which tells me. I wipe my face, and wait. And wait.

'We have to leave,' Rafael insists.

'It's not that simple, is it?

Rafael kneels down beside me and peers down into the waters of the cove. The tide is rising.

'If the mafia or the people who sent that helicopter find us, we are dead,' he says quietly.

It is a real blessing to simultaneously patronised by two different species of know-all.

35

A quiet bleep on the laptop. New message from Calypso. Rafael and I read the words on the screen as they appear. We have never seen such a long communication from either Calypso or Steve.

'Bad things happen to a dolphin who is ripped from his pod when he is only a baby. He grows up as only half a being. We are not born dolphins, we become dolphins. We learn from our mother and from our pod. Just like you humans learn from your parents. We learn to hunt and find food, we learn about the sea, we learn about friendship, we learn how to defend ourselves, we learn to talk and to listen and to use echolocation, we learn about life and death, we learn to play. We learn who we are. We become dolphins.'

'This is something I have not told your father, though he may have guessed. Steve has been a killer for a long time. When we were all prisoners in the shallow hot sea. Steve and I had the job of finding enemy divers. If we spotted an intruder we swam back to base and told our trainer. This was how we started to communicate with Michel. Together we found a language for up and down, left and right. We found ways to talk with each other about distance, colour, and water depth.'

'One evening we were on the reef. We were ambushed by two divers armed with harpoon guns. The first harpoon hit me, passing through my flukes. Steve came to help me. There was not time to return to base. He attacked the divers like we attack sharks, driving his beak hard into one diver's belly. The diver curled up into a ball. The second diver attacked. Steve was too fast and very angry. He struck the second diver again and again. Swimming so hard. Smashing the diver's chest with his beak. I called for him to stop but he was not listening.'

Calypso's dorsal fin emerges momentarily. She is swimming slowly, her clicks and whistles clearly audible.

'The two divers were dead. Steve was jaw clapping and clicking, saying bad things at the bodies as they sank to the seabed. He swam round them in tight circles, hitting them with his flukes, daring them to move. When I approached he turned on me, threatening me. I moved away and waited at a safe distance for him to calm down. I waited a long time that evening.'

'I knew that if we did not return to the base a search party would come to find us. Maybe your Dad, maybe someone else. I swam slowly towards Steve, calling out his name, trying to calm him. He ignored me until I was close then he turned, ready to attack. I held still, talking to him. Finally he relaxed. Together we pushed the dead divers and wedged them beneath the rocks. If we didn't do this, the dead divers would float to the surface. We used our flukes to shift sand up over the bodies until they were hidden and we returned to the base.'

Calypso's head emerges again and finally I can talk back.

'Dad never knew?' I sign.

'We never told him. This was not the only time that Steve killed humans. He is dangerous and I am afraid for him and for us. When he kills he goes crazy and disappears, sometimes for days. Steve has also killed dolphins. I should have told Michel the first time. I made a bad decision. And now I must find Steve and bring him back. Do you understand, Sam?'

'I understand.'

'And I must protect the baby we have rescued, to stop her becoming like Steve. The dolphins we saved are from my pod.'

'But if they are from the same pod, that means that Calypso and Steve must come from near here, doesn't it?' Rafael says. 'Ask her. Does she know this place? Does she know where we could go to be safe?'

I sense a presence behind me. Fred and Keisha are standing side by side wrapped together in a large blanket.

'Is Calypso all right?' Fred asks.

'Calypso is fine, but we are in a difficult situation. We have to leave but Steve is missing and Calypso wants to look after the dolphins we released from the nets. One is injured and the other is only a baby.'

As I speak the water ripples behind me and the children's eyes grow wide. Just a few metres from the boat are not one dorsal fin but two. I panic. Has Steve returned? Should I send the children inside? A third dorsal fin emerges, and a fourth. The smallest belongs to the dolphin calf we have rescued, who looks to be less than a metre and a half long. We form a row along the gunwale.

‘Oh, what? That is so cute!’ Keisha squeaks, clutching the sides of her face.

I didn’t really look at the calf when we were cutting the net, too many things to think about.

‘It’s a she,’ I say. ‘And that is her mother.’

‘Does she eat fish?’ Fred signs.

‘Yes,’ Calypso announces via the laptop screen. ‘She has teeth. They steal our calves as soon as they can eat fish.’

‘At about three months old,’ Rafael observes. ‘I read it somewhere.’

For a few minutes we forget all our worries and gaze down in wonder. It has stopped raining and the wind has dropped. Like us, Calypso seems to relax a little, happy to show off her protégés.

‘Looks like she’s forming her own pod,’ I say to Rafael.

‘What’s a pod?’ Keisha asks.

‘It’s a group of dolphins who all live together.’

‘How many are there in a pod?’

‘Anything from five or six to hundreds.’

We continue watching the dolphins. The calf is becoming increasingly confident and playful and Calypso is plainly enjoying the calf’s company.

‘That’s us then, isn’t it?’ Keisha says, grabbing my hand and looking up at me. ‘Pod. Me and Fred, you and Rafa, Calypso and Steve and the baby and the others. Like a row of peas. All for one and one for all, know what I mean? We are a pod.’

‘Yes, I suppose so.’ I give her a hug while trying to imagine a row of peas as heroic sword waving musketeers. ‘I suppose we are.’

I wonder if our pod will survive any longer than Calypso’s.

‘What’s Rafa doing?’

Distracted by the cuteness of the calf, I haven’t noticed Rafael climb down the ladder and into the dinghy. He paddles towards the beach followed by the injured dolphin. In the shallow water, the dolphin beaches itself on its side, allowing Rafael to look at his injured flipper. It doesn’t take long to see what has happened. Carefully and very gently Rafael cuts something on or close to the dolphin’s flipper, then unwinds what I assume must be a length of fishing line which has cut deeply into the flesh at the shoulder. When he has finished unravelling and removing the fishing line, Rafael rubs cream into the wound. The dolphin flinches agitatedly and wriggles away to deeper water.

‘The tube says it’s an anti-sceptic, anti-inflamatory, antibiotic,’ Rafael says, catching Keisha and I staring down at him. ‘anti-everything, basically. I suppose it must sting.’

‘We don’t need your medicine, our bodies heal fast,’ Calypso says. ‘Removing the wire was good.’

‘Is it a boy dolphin?’ Keisha asks.

I notice that Keisha is playing with Rafael’s phone, yet again.

‘Yes,’ I answer without, in fact, having the faintest idea. That’s one of the great things about becoming sixteen, you become an adult know-it-all, just like that. ‘And put that phone back inside. It isn’t yours.’

Keisha stomps off.

‘And take the battery out or we’ll eat you for breakfast. On toast.’

Rafael paddles the dinghy back towards the boat.

‘Can you take your phone off Keisha? How many times do I have to …’

‘You could do it.’

A flurry of clicks to my right. ‘Sam. Sam.’

Turning towards Calypso, I remember what Rafael said earlier.

‘Do you come from near here?’ I sign. ‘If these dolphins are from your pod then …’

‘I do not know,’ the reply appears on the laptop.

‘Have you asked the baby’s mother where they come from?’

‘That is not the baby’s mother, they always kill the mother.’

Great, make me look stupid, thanks. Good job Keisha is inside.

‘I’ve got an idea,’ Rafael says, climbing back aboard.

‘It’ll pass.’

He ignores my remark. ‘Why don’t we ask Calypso if the dolphins we have saved could guide us back to where they come from? It would get us away from here and it might take her home.’

I have to admit that isn’t a bad idea. I put it to Calypso. She is considering it when a fifth dorsal fin appears in the entrance to the cove.

36

Calypso shepherds the rescued dolphins round to the other side of the boat then heads towards the cove entrance.

The hydrophone is picking up a cacophony of over-lapping clicks and squeaks that the software cannot translate. It has to be Steve. Two dorsal fins race across the swelling waters of the cove before disappearing beneath the surface, only to re-emerge somewhere else. From our vantage point it looks like there is a great deal of pushing and shoving going on.

'Time to go back inside,' I urge Fred. 'Can you check that Keisha has dismantled that phone?'

'Why?' Fred demands. 'Are they fighting?'

'Of course not. Please, Fred, now.'

He trudges backwards towards the cabin door, craning his neck to see the water. On the threshold he hovers.

'Close the door and go to sleep,' I sign.

I am so tired. It feels like half my life has passed since Dad offered me that cup of hot chocolate before dawn less than twenty hours ago.

All at once I remember. My heart sinks faster and further than a bathysphere descending into the Mariana Trench. In the garden at Hotel Montefiore I made Dad a promise.

'The time, Rafael? What's the time?'

'It says on the laptop.'

'Just tell me!'

Nonplussed, he looks down and reads the screen. 'One twenty five.'

'Brilliant. Epic fail.' I spit the words out, kicking the gunwale.

'Now what?'

'Shut up,' I shout. 'Where's your phone?'

'You know where it is,' Rafael lashes back. 'You just sent Keisha inside with it.'

I throw the cabin door open so hard that it smacks against the wall, smashing the window, a rattling the windows. I am too late, how could I be so stupid?

Rafael's mobile is on the table, the battery beside it. Through the open hatch by the wheel I see down to where Keisha and Fred have settled down, back to back on one of the berths. I ram the battery into the phone.

I have missed not one but two calls. It is over seven hours since I should first have phoned. And now I have forgotten a second time. I want to hurl the phone across the cabin or, better still, toss it into the sea.

We synchronised watches at one seventeen, twelve hours and eight minutes ago. Dad will have switched on his phone for a few seconds, found I could not be reached and switched it off again. So I'm an idiot and that's that.

No, Sam, now you've started, finish the job.

Convinced I am wasting my time, I press the red icon and power up the phone, looking at my watch to count the seconds as the software boots, cursing under my breath. Nine minutes late now. The hourglass icon turns slowly then the screen display activates. Before the contact list starts loading, the phone rings.

I don't remember Dad's number but I know that the number displayed on the screen is not right. Rafael's face appears in the doorway.

'What country is 0032?'

'Belgium,' he answers. 'Why?'

'Guess. You're the genius. Should I answer it? Is it some girlfriend you forgot to tell me about?'

'I don't know.' He spins on his heel and disappears from view.

Four rings already. I have to decide. Most people hold on for six or seven rings before hanging up. It can't be Dad. Five rings. Who is it? How do they have this number? Does Rafael know who it is? Six rings. Even if he does, who rings at half past one in the morning? If I answer I will have to be ready to switch off as soon as … Seven rings.

'Are you going to answer that?' Rafael is back in the cabin doorway, his expression hard and cold.

I swallow. It is too late. People always hang up after … Rafael steps into the cabin towards me … and I press the green phone icon.

'Hello?' I say, expecting the dialling tone.

'Ah, Sam. We don't have long. You missed a call.'

'Who is this?' A bead of sweat runs down my back like a raindrop on a window.

'... and you ran away before we could finish our conversation. Though, given the circumstances ...'

Sven.

'What's happened to my parents? If they are dead I swear I will find you and kill you.'

'Come on, Sam, you aren't a killer. Besides, your parents are safe, I swear. The maître d' in the hotel, the fat man with a face like a chipmunk, he was very helpful. Your mum and dad are in a private hospital, away from prying eyes. Now listen carefully. Your dad told me to remind you to go to France. Where are you?'

'Back at the fish pens off Montecristo.'

'Why? No, don't answer that. There isn't time.'

'Do you know who Vikki Gutner is?' I ask.

Silence at the other end of the line.

'Hello? Hello?'

'Why do you ask?'

'She arrived an hour ago.'

'Where is she?'

'Handcuffed to her helicopter.'

'Get away. Don't stop to think. Whatever you are doing, leave. Didn't they tell you about 3-Tec on the train from Brussels?'

Now I recall where I heard the name 3-Tec; Z told us about them, the day this mad adventure started.

'If you want to live, leave now and head for Corsica. Switch your phone on again in six hours.'

'Wait, I want to speak with my dad.'

But the line is dead.

'So, how are your parents?' Rafael is still standing in the doorway.

'Have you been listening?'

'Why shouldn't I?'

'You have no idea what this feels like.'

Something snaps in Rafael. 'Two weeks ago, just before Christmas, my dad was pushed out a helicopter and killed. You were with him, have you forgotten that?' he shouts. 'And I haven't seen or spoken with my mother for a long time. And how about that little girl asleep on the boat who has just lost her dad and her grandmother? What gives you the monopoly on suffering, Sam?

'It's not the same. You don't understand.'

'No, Sam, it's like Calypso said, you don't understand. We don't stand a chance unless we all support each other, no matter what, and that means you realising that you are not the only person on the planet.'

I want to shout back but somehow, for once, I manage to shut up.

I just stand there. And stand some more, staring at nothing in particular, clenching and unclenching my jaw. Rafael is right. At least my parents are alive, and together. I've been behaving like a total donk for days, jealous whenever Rafael and Dad seemed to be getting along, determined to exclude him from the family reunion at the hotel, doing everything I can to push him away. What is the matter with me?

'I'm sorry,' I say finally. 'You miss your parents as much as I do.'

'My dad was a bastard, but he was still my dad.'

'I've been horrible to Keisha too. All her stupid questions. Winding me up with that rubbish about you and me and true lurve … and all that. But she's only nine. What does she know about anything?'

'Yes. She's only nine.' Rafael stares at the floor. 'What does she know?'

Then he looks at me.

And that is the first time I see it in his eyes.

How could I have been so blind and self-absorbed? And I keep being sarcastic about his empathy skills? I call him an emotional pygmy? Embarrassed, I look down at the two children huddled side by side on one of the berths. Fred is fast asleep, but Keisha is staring back at me, small and frightened. She understands people better than I do. Everyone does..

'We need to talk with Calypso and Steve.' Rafael changes the subject. 'We have to sort this out and work together.'

'I've been so horrible. And so stupid.'

'You're stressed. We all are. Come on.' He gives me a clumsy pat on the shoulder, like we are mates on a football team.

Which makes me feel even worse.

We step outside. It is clear that, far from being resolved, the argument between Calypso and Steve is still in full swing, with the barrage of noise picked up by the hydrophone blaring out of both the laptop and the loudspeaker mounted outside the cabin. Two dorsal fins scythe back and forth cross the waters of the cove, accompanied by occasional leaps and fluke slaps. We cross the deck to check on the other dolphins and find them exactly where Calypso left them, tucked up against the boat and barely moving. Their body language is clear, they are frightened.

I have had enough of all the arguing. Grabbing my face mask and snorkel from inside the cabin, I pull off my anorak and jumper, kick off my shoes, ask Rafael to turn on the search light, and I jump overboard.

37

From the moment the lights first appear on the south western horizon, Paolo knows he is in trouble. Still tied to one of the upright posts around the sixth fish pen, it has been forty minutes since he regained consciousness and in that time he has not seen a single dolphin come up for air. There are only two explanations; either they are all dead or they have all escaped.

Either way he is finished. Yesterday they lost a million euros worth of tuna, and now he is responsible for a further loss. No sign of his colleague Stefano since he disappeared underwater with the other diver, and Paolo assumes he must be dead. With little over half an hour to go before the two ships reach shore, Paolo knows he too will be a dead man if he hasn't disappeared by the time the ships arrive.

Thirty minutes of wriggling have failed to loosen his ropes but now he applies himself with renewed vigour. The girl, he is sure it was a girl in spite of her height and the dry suit, tied him while he was unconscious. She has done a thorough job, there is very little play in any of the knots. With his arms tied behind his back and then to the bottom of the post he can hardly move his torso, nor can he bring his hands close to his feet to attack the knots around his ankles. His spirits rise when he feels his penknife in his trouser pocket but, when he finally manages to push it out, it turns out to be a pack of chewing gum.

Maybe if he tries sitting up. He rolls onto his shoulder and he pushes his hands back towards the post, feeling a tiny amount of up and down play in the rope. Pulling his feet under his backside, he tries to throw himself up onto his knees. Three times his shoulder leaves the boards of the walkway only to crash back down. He shifts his weight, rolling round and tensing his thighs, then tries again. This time he has more momentum. His body lifts higher and he finds himself kneeling with his hands resting on his heels.

Flexing and unflexing his fingers to increase the blood flow, Paolo looks over his shoulder. The lights are closer, the ships are probably only three or four kilometres away. Eight minutes maybe less to get away. He feels the knots around his ankles with his fingertips and sets to work, forcing the nylon cord against itself.

One minute later his feet are free. If he can stand up, the pressure on his hands will diminish because the post narrows just a little towards the top. He guesses right and as he climbs to his feet the ropes that secure his hands to the post slacken enough for him to start teasing loose the knots around his wrists. He is free.

Throwing himself into the water, Paolo swims the two hundred metres to the beach, his muscles cramping painfully as arms and legs that have been bound together for well over an hour struggle to function. By the time he reaches the shingle, the ships' engines are loud and clear at his back. With no time to waste, he races up the beach in the darkness and keeps on going, scrambling up the rocks as fast as his fifty year old bones and aching legs will carry him.

38

The prow of our boat is pushing a course through the heavy undulating swell. Like ice skating across bread dough, I imagine. We are out of sight of land with nothing but the sea for company but I wonder if we are any further from Montecristo now than we were ten minutes ago.

The rigging clicks in a stiff breeze. Back in dry clothes and finally beginning to warm up after my reckless midnight swim in the cold waters of the cove wearing only jeans and a t-shirt, I am drinking a cup of hot chocolate while fixing Rafael's broken scuba gear.

Rafael is at the wheel and we are heading east, using the ship's compass rather than the GPS.

'Seven knots. It shouldn't take more than four or five hours, if we don't have to stop too often.' Rafael turns to look at me. 'Oh come on, Sam. So now you know. I understand that you don't feel anything at all for me and I am big enough to get over it, OK? Eventually.'

'I suppose so,' I answer feebly. I haven't spoken since we left the cove. I feel awkward and uncomfortable. How can he have feelings for me? What have I done to deserve them? Why does everything have to be so complicated?

'Good,' Rafael speaks matter-of-factly. 'So, tell me why Steve suddenly became a pussycat. What did you say to him?'

'Nothing much.'

Rafael sighs and starts to turn away.

'I didn't say anything. Not to start with. He and Calypso were shouting at each other and I barged in between them and gave Steve a hug, that's all. Then I told them both what Keisha had said, that we were now a pod and that meant we all stuck together, no matter what. I said that stuff happens in life that you can't explain. You just have to run with it.' It is all tumbling out of me in a rush, just like it did earlier. 'Our lives have a purpose, even if we don't always understand why. We have a chance to change the world. It's only a small chance but it is a chance and we have to take it because if we don't then that's it, gone forever.'

'Wow. Nothing too heavy then.'

'And Calypso doesn't trust Steve either. She is worried he will lose it and attack the other dolphins if they get in his way. We have to stop by the way,' I say, checking my watch.

We have promised to stop every twenty minutes to check that the calf and the injured dolphin are keeping up. As luck would have it we guessed right; when Calypso said home to the rescued female she went west, which was exactly where we want to go. Problem sorted. For now.

Rafael closes the throttle and the engine hum dies down. Carrying the largest torch, I step out on deck, walk to the stern and shine the light onto the water. Even with a thick fleece, I shiver in the chilling sea breeze blowing from the west. Five beaks appear above the waves.

'Everything OK?' I sign.

'Yes.' Calypso clicks.

'We are doing well. We should arrive before sunrise,' I sign back.

Seeing the face of the calf peering up is magical. I give a thumbs up and go back inside. Rafael opens the throttle and we set off again. He is developing a nasty cough. Watching him, I realise I am actually quite annoyed with the way he is able to switch off his supposed feelings for me. Just like that. They obviously aren't very serious. Not that I care. I wonder if he really understands that I don't see him that way.

'Rafael, I was thinking that maybe I ought to …

'Grab some sleep?' Rafael suggests. 'Good idea. I'll call you in an hour.'

'Yeah. OK.'

That went well. Stick to the day job, Sam. I find a blanket and lie down on one of the benches. Within seconds I am asleep.

39

Paolo sits on a boulder to catch his breath. He is two hundred metres above the beach, having scrambled up between tumbled and jagged rocks.

Montecristo is a nature reserve, about eleven square kilometres in area. The further he runs the more Paolo becomes aware of the impossibility of escape. It is twenty kilometres to the next island, Isola Pianosa, and thirty or more to the Italian mainland. In another fifty minutes he will reach the top of the island. Then what? There is no town, no-one to help, no-one to hold hostage. There were two nature reserve keepers when the mafia ships first arrived, but a gang was dispatched to murder both men and smash their boats to ensure news of the tuna pens didn't leak out.

There is water but no food. Not in January. Without a knife he will struggle to catch anything. He cannot even make traps to catch seabirds. The lizards are all hibernating and his chances of catching one of the wild goats they have seen from the ships are practically zero.

His wet clothes are clinging to him and, with the air getting colder the higher he climbs, Paolo needs to find shelter if he is to survive the night. The island has been a prison for good reason; they won't send anyone after him, they don't have to. They will simply leave him to die.

He beats his arms around his body and jumps up and down to get the blood circulating. To his right the land falls away into a valley with large bushes. Maybe there are trees down there, or an abandoned building. After a last look down towards the bay, where the two ships have now dropped anchor, Paolo sets off. Within a few steps his ankle twists over in a rut left by grazing goats and he tumbles downward, rolling into a gorse bush thick with spikes. Howling in agony, head buzzing, Paolo picks himself up and hobbles slowly down the steep slope, reaching a hand behind him to steady himself.

Nestling further down in the cleft of the valley is a forest. He has guessed correctly. Slipping and sliding in the mud, he glimpses of the sea far below and see something else that both surprises him and lifts his spirits. He plainly isn't the only person on the island.

A broken sapling serves as an improvised walking stick, taking the weight off his rapidly swelling ankle. The sea is no longer visible, but Paolo knows that as long as he keeps heading downward he is heading in the right direction. He pushes into the darkness of the forest, low hanging branches clawing at his shirt, brushing his face, narrowly missing his left eye. Cursing aloud, he feels his eyelid. Blood gathers quickly on his eyelashes then drips into his eye, viscous and oily, blurring his vision. Beneath the trees the odour of damp vegetation hangs in the air, tangible and cloying.

Loose stones hide treacherously beneath the moss and dead leaves and Paolo is obliged to move cautiously, testing every step before transferring his weight to his throbbing ankle. On reaching a large flat rock he picks up speed, eager to get out from under the trees. Almost too late he notices the void loitering beyond the lip of the rock. He stops mid-step, grabbing a tree trunk to halt his forward momentum. Some five metres below him, an animal senses his presence and hurries away in the darkness in a rush of footsteps and cracking braches.

Paolo picks his way left, skirting the overhanging and continuing downward. Eventually odour of humid earth and rotting leaves is replaced by a more acrid scent, the smell of burning. He saw the fire on the hill from the boat and knows where he must be. Slowly now, he does not want to advertise his arrival. Checking that the coast is clear, Paolo emerges from under the trees and crosses over to the smouldering trunk, his feet crunching on the charcoal remains of burnt bushes and shrubs. From his vantage point above the bay he has a perfect view of the fish pens and the ships. How many of them were up here earlier on the hill looking down? The two divers and one or two to light the fire, or were there more?

Down below there is activity on the deck of the Serena. A group of men are pulling something along. The faintest sound of shouting reaches him. He doesn't know all the men on all three ships ships but he knows what they are pulling. It is Vittorio, the old man, being dragged by the shirt towards the back of the boat. Paolo doesn't need to see what happens next. Crouching down low, he hurries down the slope away from the bay. Out of the darkness the ruins of a building appear but Paolo is no longer interested in finding shelter, he has bigger plans. He comes to a stop only when he reaches the top of a cliff overlooking a small cove.

He is right, it is a helicopter, but it is smaller than he expected. Room for two or three people, if that. Why haven't they left yet?

The only way into the cove is down the narrow path to his left. Without a moon the night is dark and the cliff shades the path from what little light there is in the sky. Paolo has to hope he can approach unnoticed, ambush the occupants and force them to take him with them. Making his way down the path, sliding on his injured ankle, he is convinced they will hear him and shoot and yet he reaches the bottom without seeing any sign of life. Could they have abandoned the helicopter? It won't help him if they have; Paolo has never even sat in a plane let alone piloted an aircraft of any kind. He crosses the narrow beach, flinching with every dry snap and crack of the shifting shingle, glad he has a big stick, wishing he had a gun. A safe distance from the helicopter he stops.

There are no lights on in the cockpit. The glass-domed front is like a globule of oil floating in a stew but, in the shadow beneath the cockpit, he sees movement. Something large and long. A seal perhaps?

Stick raised, Paolo advances slowly. Whatever it is beneath the helicopter it isn't moving now. In all likelihood it is just seaweed lifted by the breeze or beached flotsam. He has allowed his imagination to get away with him.

'Stop!'

They must have seen him when he was still at the top of the cliff and hidden in wait. He is trapped.

'Put the stick down and come forward very slowly.'

A woman's voice, speaking good Italian. Is she the one he attacked at the fish pen? He drops the stick and shuffles forwards. Now she is moving he can make out her shape more clearly. She is lying along one of the runners the helicopter is resting on. Why hasn't she stood up?

'Stop. Listen carefully. I need your help. I want you to open the left hand door of the helicopter and tilt the seat forward.'

He understands. The woman cannot come out from under the helicopter. She is shackled to it and looks tired and weak. Paolo feels an overwhelming surge of hatred and anger and the desire to kick her to pieces to pay her back for what happened at the fish pen. His ugly gap-toothed grin spreads across his face as he leans forward and peers down.

'Listen to me,' the woman says. 'I can fly this machine. Without me you are stuck here.'

His grin fades, how has she guessed what he needs?

'Calm down,' she says. 'Do as I ask and together we leave this island.'

'You steal my dolphins. You leave me tied to the empty fish pen like a leg of ham hanging in a shop, and now I must help you?'

'That was someone else. They have already gone. I am a victim like you.'

Paolo is confused. How many different groups of people are there on this supposedly deserted island?

'Under the left hand seat is a toolbox. Bring it to me.'

The desire to get away is stronger than the desire to hurt her, but only just. Once she has flown him to Elba or the mainland, once the helicopter has touched down safely, then he will beat her to a pulp. He straightens up, pulls open the helicopter door. The seat tips forward to reveal a wide shallow box of tools. And a torch. He takes the box and places it on the ground

On his hands and knees, he inspects how the woman is shackled. Handcuffs. One set have been used to secure her left ankle to the metal skid. She has both wrists in the other set of cuffs, which have been looped around the vertical bar.

He doesn't need to be told which tools to use. He attacks the weakest link with the long pincers. The woman groans weakly as he pulls and twists the cuffs securing her wrists. He ignores her. The link breaks and her hands fall back on the sand. Her eyes are closed. In the torchlight he sees how tired she is and wonders whether she will be capable of standing, never mind piloting a helicopter. Maybe there is water in the cabin.

He turns his attention to the second set of handcuffs, dragging the torch round to shine its beam on her ankle. He has the pincers in place, biting on the link that holds the two cuffs together, when they flinch against the skid bar.

And that is all the warning Paolo gets.

As he pulls his head back, a spanner smashes down against the back of his skull with a sickening crunch and he goes out like a spent match.

Vikki Gutner pushes the body away from her. With both hands free, it won't take long to crush the link that holds her ankle to the skid bar. Why are people so stupid?

40

I awake with a start, my legs falling off the bench, snatching at the table top to steady myself. The boat is in almost total darkness. Aside from Fred's occasional snoring and the intermittent creaking of the hull, a heavy silence envelopes everything like a thick blanket of ice.

Why aren't the engines running? Where is Rafael? What has woken me?

The boat is rocking in the swell. I stand up, keeping the blanket wrapped around my shoulders. Senses on high alert, I stagger across the cabin to the wheel, jarring my feet as the sharp upwards and downwards movement of the boat brings the floor to meet my feet too early or too late. I carefully pull open the drawer to take the gun we seized from the woman.

The drawer is empty.

It is as dark outside as inside. Through the windows I can barely see where the boat ends and the sea begins. I want to call out but sense it would be dangerous.

'Sam?' said a small voice whispers from the berths down below.

'Keisha. Shh.'

'What's happening? I feel sick.'

'Don't move. I'm going outside.'

'I'm scared.'

So am I, I want to say. 'It's OK,' I say instead. 'Stay down there and keep an eye on Fred, I'll be back in a minute.'

I pull open the cabin door and step outside.

'Lie down!'

It is Rafael's voice.

'Where are you?' I hiss.

'Aft. Get down now.'

I drop to the deck. The sea is rising up like a wall above the boat then falling away then rising again.

'What is …'

'Another boat.'

I crawl on my hands and knees towards the back of the boat and find Rafael crouched behind the crate, peering out into the darkness, pistol in hand.

He puts his fingers to his lips then cups his ear. I do the same. Above the noise of the wind and liquid notes of the water caressing the hull is another sound, the distant rumbling chug of an engine.

'I don't think they've noticed us,' Rafael whispers in my ear. 'Steve warned me when we stopped ten minutes ago. The dolphins had heard another engine, so I switched everything off, lights, engine, everything. They are less than forty metres away, with all their lights on. I think they are fishermen.'

'There, can you see?'

The hull of a boat about twice the size of ours is briefly visible before we dip down into another trough.

'Did you ask Steve or Calypso to go a take a look?'

'I can't, Sam, my sign language isn't good enough.'

'What were you going to do with that?' I point at the gun in his hand. 'Storm aboard them and take them all hostage?'

'No hostages. I'll make them all walk the plank and then I take their treasure.'

We laugh quietly. It releases the tension. The engine noise is getting fainter.

'They're heading south, I think,' Rafael says. 'Another five minutes then I'll start her up.'

'Start her up? Aye aye, Cap'n. You'll be covering your arms in tattoos next, shouting Yo ho ho, and wearing a parrot on your shoulder.'

'Don't forget the eye patch.'

'iPatch? Does that come with fancy apps?

I go inside to check up on the young ones. Fred is still snoring. I promise Keisha a hot drink as soon as it is safe to light a burner.

'With milk this time?'

'There's only water.'

By the time Rafael comes inside, Keisha and I are huddled together under my blanket sitting at the table. He starts the engine, and checks the compass heading by torchlight.

'I'm switching on the GPS for a minute,' he announces. 'We've drifted.'

'Are we there yet?' Keisha asks.

'We've stopped eight times so we must be three quarters of the way.'

'Eight times?'

'You looked tired, Sam.' Rafael coughs and wheezes.

'She needs her beauty sleep, that one.'

'Shut up, Keisha.'

'I'm only …'

'Don't bother.'

Keisha looks like she is ready for an argument then she changes tack.

'Where are we going?' she asks.

'France,' I say, at the same time as Rafael says, 'Corsica.'

Before either of us can explain, the boat is smacked hard on the starboard side. A huge glancing blow is followed by a high-pitched scraping along the length of the boat, like screeching fingernails along a blackboard. Keisha screams and so do I, but we can hardly hear ourselves above the noise. Everything that isn't nailed in place crashes downwards and rolls across the floor, which is now at a twenty or thirty degree angle. From within a cupboard comes the metallic ring of crashing pots, pans and crockery. Rafael clings desperately to the wheel trying to pull the boat away from whatever is locked against it.

We can't have run aground, unless we have come across a rock sticking up out of the sea. It has to be a vessel of some kind. Has the mafia caught up with us? Are they ramming us?

The door down to the berths slams shut with a massive bang. Two seconds later, lit in a ghostly glow that is suddenly pouring into the cabin through the windows from outside, the door is pushed open and Fred's terrified face appears.

'There's water falling on the beds' he signs.

Like that is the biggest of our worries I think, then panic as I realise that if water is coming in below deck we are in desperate trouble.

The boat is juddering so hard it will surely be shaken to pieces. We are being pushed under the waves, water is streaming into the cabin under the door, and there is nothing we can do. Fred half runs, half staggers across to me. I draw him close, clinging hold of him and Keisha with all my strength.

It looks as if our luck has finally run out.

41

Major Tenebris gazes at the photo of the giant spider crab on the wall behind his desk while quietly whistling his favourite tune, O Fortuna from Carmina Burana.

It is dark, relentless, music that builds like the pressure of hot magma beneath the cap of a volcano. Tenebris loves the Latin words, sung by a huge choir, because it describes himself and the power he has over others.

Sors immanis et inanis, rota tu volubilis, status malus …

Fate, monstrous and empty, you whirling wheel, and evil state …

Adult Japanese spider crabs are monsters, with a leg span of over four metres. Diving in a bathysphere off the coast of Okinawa, when Tenebris was still serving in a regular navy, they found the giant crab, one hundred and fifty metres down. The image has stayed with him, even without the photo on his office wall. In a robotic ballet, the crab had crawled mechanically across the sand on long striped legs and surrounded a starfish, its legs forming a cage of prison bars from which there could be no escape.

As the bathysphere began its journey back to the surface and the seabed was once again plunged into total darkness, Tenebris decided that he had witnessed the perfect metaphor for absolute power; surround those you seek to control, let them understand that there is no possibility of escape then tear them apart limb by limb at your leisure.

Why then, he asks himself for the twentieth time, has he taken his eye off the ball with regard to the hunt for Michel Blanchard? Watching Messi and Watson on the helipad clambering aboard the helicopter, an hour earlier, he saw the fear in their eyes, they know that if they fail again they are dead men. Which is how it should be.

In truth, though neither man knows it, they will die even if they do succeed in their mission, but men without hope do not act so that final truth is hidden from them.

Tenebris knows he has misjudged Gutner, not because she has no intention of carrying out the task she has taken on herself but because there is something she fears more than she fears him and that makes her unreliable. He has allowed himself a moment's sympathy for her, bullied as she has been by the envy of less able colleagues. Sentiment is a poor aid to decision making.

Tenebris understood that Vikki Gutner would fail when they spoke earlier on the phone. It was clear from the tone of her voice that she will hesitate when the moment demands action and, regardless of the promise he made to her that she has until midday to capture or kill her target, he has decided that she must be terminated and that her job must pass to Messi and Watson.

A knock on the door.

'Yes.'

The door opens to reveal a young woman member of the support staff. At the same moment the red telephone rings. Tenebris picks it up.

'I have a phone call for you. The caller says ...'

'I said no calls except from …'

'He says you want to hear from him, Sir. Code words: Batinah Highway.'

Tenebris holds his hand up to the woman at the door.

'Your plane, Sir, is ready to …'

Covering the receiver with his hand, he cuts her off, 'I know. Wait.' He moves his hand away and speaks into the phone. 'Put him through'

'Lorenzo,' says the voice at the other end of the line.

It is him. Without even being aware of the gesture, Tenebris's left hand lifts to his cheek. His fingertips follow the rough outline of the scar that has permanently disfigured his face, the wound that cost him an eye. The man who betrayed him and left him for dead on a desert road in Oman four years ago has reappeared.

'Coemans,' Tenebris says.

'Call me Pim, Lorenzo.'

'What do you want, Coemans?'

'This is about what you want.'

'Go on.'

'Instead of hunting children, why don't you and I sort this out mano a mano, to coin a phrase? I can deliver Blanchard senior and his technology for a price.'

How can Coemans be involved? It makes no sense. The man vanished off the face of the earth. Three intelligence agencies have failed to track him down..

'Are you there?'

'How do I know it isn't already too late, Coemans? My interest in Blanchard ends as soon as he and his discovery becomes public knowledge.'

'You have my word.'

'Your word?' Tenebris splutters incredulously.

'OK, forget my word. One of your operatives attempted to apprehend Sam Blanchard and the Santoni boy less than two hours ago on the island of Montecristo. Correct?'

Tenebris grunts his acceptance of this fact.

'Do you know Bastia?'

Silence.

'In Corsica.'

'I know where Bastia is,' Tenebris snarls.

'Bar Chez Jules in the old harbour, nine o'clock. I'll buy you breakfast.'

The line is cut off.

Tenebris glances at the photo on his wall. Who is the spider crab and who the starfish now? He motions to the woman at the door to come and collect his briefcase then pushes past her and out into the corridor.

Hundreds of kilometres away, the man known to Tenebris as Pim Coemans savours the pleasure of being called by a name he hasn't used for four years.

42

Calypso swims back and forth in a state of extreme agitation, while Steve, the calf and the female dolphin wait patiently. Beside them, hanging in the water, is the body of the injured dolphin. Already traumatised by the injury to his flipper the young male panicked when the ship appeared and crashed into La Vita Nuova. Instead of swimming down and away from the ship he swam straight up only to be crushed between the two vessels.

La Vita Nuova's engines are running but the boat is still drifting, and listing to one side. Calypso swims along the boat's starboard bow, her echolocation quickly identifying a long and deep scratch that runs from one end of the boat to the other. The hull has cracked and Calypso has seen enough of boats to know that, left unrepaired, the vessel will sink. They have to reach shore as soon as possible.

Calypso emerges from the relative calm below the waves into the noisy chaos above, with its biting wind and surging swell that buffets the listing boat. It has started to rain again, thick driving rain that peppers her skin.

There is no sign of anyone on deck. She clicks and whistles to draw Sam and Rafael's attention. Behind her, the others surface briefly for air before disappearing back beneath the surging swell. Calypso calls again and again, becoming increasingly worried. She leaps up out of the water, high enough to see that the cabin door is shut before crashing back down into the water.

The female clicks and whistles anxiously, the calf quiet beside her. Calypso brushes gently against the calf, lifting him and comforting him. Maybe the humans are all dead. Maybe they are trapped. If they are trapped then there is little the dolphins can do to help. She can throw herself onto the boat to draw their attention, but if they are unable to respond or help her back into the sea she will die there on the deck.

Somehow … somehow … All at once she realises what she must try to do.

43

Dad is turning the huge wheel in the centre of the outer door while I watch. The wheel makes high-pitched shrieks as it turns, metal pulling against metal, until he can turn it no further. He crosses past me to the second door and starts to turn its wheel in the opposite direction. As the wheel spins it clicks rapidly, as if on a ratchet.

Dad pulls open the door to reveal, sunk into the floor, the moon pool in which a dozen tiny and beautiful sharks are swimming. In the soft glow, men and women in white lab coats walk back and forth, clipboards in hand. I can't hear their whispered words clearly because, I realise, the room is underwater and the open air is now all in the moon pool in which the sharks are flying like birds of prey soaring on thermals high above a mountain.

Someone screams and I feel myself falling through the moon pool, tumbling into the depths of a darkening sky.

I open my eyes. I am back on La Vita Nuova squashed into a corner of the cabin with Fred and Keisha pressed up against me. The lights are still off and the cabin is very dark. Rain hard as nails is thumping on the roof and the cabin stinks of diesel fumes. Keisha is crying gently and Fred is fiddling with my hair. My clothes are wet through. I pull my hair away.

'Why are they screaming?' Keisha whispers.

'Who's screaming?'

'Outside.'

As she speaks a blood-chilling scream fills the air. I jerk up into a sitting position, where is Rafael? Two legs are visible not far away, hopefully attached to a body. Clinging to a table leg I drag myself to my feet. The boat is listing badly. Are we sinking?

The sloping floor rolls back and forth as I stagger towards Rafael who is on his back, asleep or unconscious. His breathing is laboured. Since I rescued him at the fish pen it has steadily got worse and I worry he has an infection. It has been a while since he had an asthma attack; I try to remember where he keeps his inhaler. Fred helps me roll Rafael over onto his side.

Then it strikes me, if it isn't Rafael screaming then who is it?

'Look after him,' I sign, hoping that Fred can see my hands in the gloom. 'I'm going outside.'

I have to kick the door hard to open it. Rain dropping from the sky in strings, drenches me from head to toe in seconds. There is still no sign of land, only the mountainous swell of the sea that we are riding like a leaf spinning along a storm drain. I am desperately thirsty.

An ugly scream rips the air. The only time I have ever heard anything like it was when a group of us watched a Japanese horror film after school one day at Daniel's house, before his dad came home from his shift; it is the sound of a torture victim. It chills me to the bone.

I cling to the door frame. A burst of clicks and whistles pulls me to my senses. Riding the swell by the boat is Calypso.

'Calypso!' I shout, waving wildly. 'What happened? Is everyone OK?' I sign. 'Who is screaming?'

Another barrage of clicks. I need to find the hydrophone and laptop. Will the hydrophone survive in this churning sea? I am stepping back into the cabin when Calypso says Sam.

As a spoken word.

I swear. I am not making this up. I turn round and she does it a second time.

'Sam.'

Open-jawed, I stare at her. How on earth is she doing it? Dolphins don't have vocal chords. They don't speak through their mouths. They don't have lips.

'How are you doing that?' I sign.

She screams. The scream that woke me up.

'Hang on a minute.' I dash inside and collect the laptop. As I lower the hydrophone into the sea the laptop starts to translate.

'I thought you had all died. The boat is badly damaged, you must get to land quickly,' the laptop screen reads.

'Have you seen the damage?'

'Two cracks. If one breaks the boat will sink, Sam.'

'OK, and are you all safe? What hit us?'

'A very large ship with many windows.'

'Our lights were off. They must have not seen us in the dark.'

‘The ship hit our injured friend. He is dead.’

‘I’m sorry, Calypso.’

‘We are very sad. Now we must go. Straight away.’

I hurry back inside. Miraculously, the engine is still running. I put the boat into forward gear, open the throttle and we start to move. Immediately the boat pulls to the right. Dad explained about adjusting the trim but I cannot remember how to do it so I pull the wheel to the left to compensate and hang on tight.

‘Keisha, look for Rafa’s inhaler. It must be in his bag.’ I shout over my shoulder.

Keisha pulls at the door to the berths until eventually it opens and she disappears below. She reappears with Rafael’s backpack and the leather backpack Sven gave me. ‘Who was screaming?’

‘Calypso. I don’t know how she’s doing it.’

‘There’s water sloshing about down there. It’s knee deep. Are we sinking?’

‘Of course not, but we need to reach land quickly.’

‘Which means we’re sinking, right?’

‘Can you find his inhaler? It’s a L-shaped grey plastic ...’

‘I know what they are, our David’s mum has one.’

If Rafael was right, we are about ten kilometres from Corsica. Less than an hour away, if we are still afloat. The compass says we are heading west.

‘Do I just shove it in his gob?’

‘No, you don’t. You wake him up gently and offer it to him.’

‘He sounds like one of them weedy motorbikes that do wheelies in Toxteth.’

Keisha crouches down next to Rafael and gently rubs his face. I am massively relieved when his eyes open. He smiles at her and takes the inhaler.

‘I’m hungry,’ Rafael announces a few seconds later.

‘What do you want me to do? Break out in cream cakes?’ Keisha answers.

Rafael responds with a coughing fit.

I feel a pull on my sleeve and find Fred beside me making big eyes and clutching a fist full of chocolates from the leather backpack.

‘Yes, those are my chocolates.’

‘Can I give some to Rafael?’ he signs.

‘OK, we’ll share two now and you can put the others back. Keisha, stop playing with Rafael’s smart phone. How many times …?’

I make myself a mental promise that when we reach Corsica we will drop Keisha and Fred off at a police station or social services or a zoo or something.

It is almost five in the morning, according to my watch. Dawn is still over two hours away.

Keisha offers me the Maltesers.

'You can have the first one,' I say. She takes one then makes to carry on. 'No, stop, I'll have that one. Don't they teach you anything in Liverpool? The second Malteser is the best one.' I take one out of the bag. 'This one is crunchier, sweeter, and more chocolatey than all the others. OK, you can have the rest.'

I pop the Malteser in my mouth and make uncontrolled yummy noises.

'You're weird big time. Like loopy fruit,' Keisha observes, making a little circles next to her temple with her index finger then pretending to pull a cloth back and forth through the space between her ears.

Whatever. She can think what she likes. Rafael is stretching, rubbing his head and sitting up. He takes the chocolate Fred offers him.

'Do you know what?' I say. 'After all that's happened in the past few hours, I've got a good feeling that all our troubles are behind us.'

'Are Maltesers even legal?' Keisha says to no-one in particular.

44

Vikki Gutner realises that she spoke too soon, calling people stupid, unless she is willing to include herself. As she swiped the fisherman across the back of the head, his body flinched uncontrollably and the pincers he was holding ended up out of reach. It has taken her the best part of ten minutes to pull apart the links holding the handcuffs together with the spanner.

Finally, she climbs to her feet and stretches and, avoiding the rather ugly mess beside the dead man's head, clambers into the helicopter. She is half-way through her pre-flight checks when she spots the headlight in the sky. It is immediately obvious that it is not a commercial flight passing by over-head and within seconds she also knows that the aircraft, presumably another helicopter, is heading straight towards her. Tenebris has double-crossed her.

Her choices are stark: a dogfight in the sky, which she will lose since her machine carries no weaponry, or a fight on the ground. She abandons the helicopter and limps across the shingle towards the path that leads up out of the cove.

Descending rapidly towards the small cove on the island of Montecristo in a six seater AS350 are Watson, Messi and their pilot. Since leaving Sicily they have stopped only briefly to re-fuel in Sardinia.

Messi is in the co-pilot's seat, Watson asleep across the back seats. While not unfamiliar with bullying, having been both victim and perpetrator at a minor public school in Oxfordshire, Timothy Watson has always found meetings with Tenebris extremely stressful. Soon after take off Watson lay down to calm his nerves. He is still sleeping as they approach the island, some three hours later, guided in by the tracking device implanted under the skin next to Gutner's collarbone.

In front of Messi is a screen fed by a technology that still fascinates him even after a decade of using it; a thermal imaging camera.

'I'm seeing movement on the ground,' Messi announces.

'Can we see her helicopter?' the pilot asks.

'No, I imagine the aircraft has had time to cool, but we are picking up two organics. One stationary, one on the move.

'Final in forty seconds.' The pilot speaks aloud on final approach as a matter of routine and not because he expects anyone to listen. 'Altitude three hundred metres. Terrain at landing area unknown but likely sand or shingle. Obstacles evident.'

'Shall I wake Watson?'

'No point. Altitude two hundred metres. Anything more on the target?'

'Both figures appear to be human. The stationary one is lying down, the other keeps disappearing and reappearing.'

'Probably vegetation. A forest perhaps. Altitude one hundred metres. Final in fifteen seconds.'

As they continue their descent the island looms higher and higher above them, a jagged jet black silhouette against a sky that is only marginally lighter.

'Do we know what armaments she is carrying?' the pilot asks.

'A hand gun, and knives possibly. She is a martial arts expert.'

The powerful headlight is now illuminating the beach of the cove, revealing the small helicopter and the figure lying beneath it.

'I can destroy the helicopter from here.'

'No, we are under instruction to interview her before completing the assignment. I would rather present this as a rescue, at least to start with.'

'Understood.'

The moving figure is above them and visible only intermittently. The thermal imaging camera is now close enough to give a temperature reading of both figures.

'The person beneath the aircraft is either hypothermic or dead. We're safe to land,' Messi says, pulling his handgun out of its shoulder holster.

'I've heard that before,' the pilot comments.

The helicopter's downdraught whips the water of the cove, sending a thick spray in all directions as the pilot picks a spot to touch down. He keeps the nose and headlight pointing straight at the other machine. As soon as the landing skids touch the shingle he cuts the power and the rotor blades slow, the engine note dropping rapidly in pitch.

The figure on the ground is not Vikki Gutner, but a large male. A display shows Gutner's tracking device is above them and to their right.

‘Timothy, we have a little job for you,’ Messi announces, prodding the sleeping Watson. ‘Wakey, wakey.’

His eyes thick with sleep, Watson stretches and looks around him.

‘Listen, old chap, a bit of a headache. Why don’t you do the little job while I find a kettle and make us a cup of something hot?’

Messi removes his headphones, pushes open his door and steps out onto the ground. Sliding back the rear door, he shakes Watson roughly.

‘No, you listen, old chap,’ Messi says sarcastically. ‘We have some climbing to do. Our target is trying to escape. Get up.’

‘I say, that’s a little disagreeable,’ Watson says as he climbs out and spots the body by the small helicopter.

‘It’s this way,’ Messi calls out over his shoulder, ‘and don’t forget that tracking unit.’

The two men slip and slide their way up the path that leads out of the cove. Besides their weapons, Messi carries a small night vision scope and Watson has the tracking unit slung on a strap around his neck. They reach the strip of burned vegetation and see the three mafia ships and fish pens all lit up in the bay below them.

‘I thought Montecristo was a nature reserve,’ Watson observes. ‘What’s that, a scout camp?’

‘She is maybe thirty metres above us,’ Messi says, having at last located Gutner with the night scope. ‘I think she may be injured.’

‘Shall I wait here? Keep an eye on that lot. We don’t want to frighten her.’

‘Nice try.’ Messi points up the steep slope.

Watson sighs and trudges into the treeline. As they climb, Messi becomes increasingly concerned about the possibility of an ambush; Gutner is no fool, unlike Watson, and she has plenty of reason to distrust them. She has fled specifically because she wants to control the context and location of their encounter. It is dark under the trees. The night scope has lost her again, it is highly possible that she is hiding.

They reach a massive rocky overhang maybe twenty metres wide. All evidence of footprints disappears. If they choose the wrong path Gutner might outfox them, make her way down to the cove and make her escape while they are still up on the mountain.

‘Can you see her?’

'Yes,' Watson says, consulting the tracking display. 'Fifteen to twenty metres.'

'We have to split up. I'll go left and you follow round to the right. I'll find you at the top. If you see anything, shout.'

Messi pulls his gun out of its holster and Watson does the same.

'That woman is a bitch. She deserves everything she gets,' Watson mutters, panting heavily from the exertion of the climb.

'Remember, we have to interrogate her.'

'Don't lecture me. I know perfectly well what we have to do.'

'And don't stop on the way,' Messi calls over his shoulder as he sets off.

Messi is quickly out of sight. The ground is steeper than before. Watson re-holsters his gun and trousers the tracking display. He crawls up the slope on his hands and knees, cursing aloud when he grabs at a stick and finds it covered in small thorns. A few more steps and Watson sits down, facing back down the hill, desperate to remove the thorns from his fingers and thumb. It is fifteen years since he has seen active service and it should be obvious to anyone that Tenebris is bang out of order sending him to chase after Gutner in the middle of the bloody night. Mindless cruelty.

He is still muttering to himself as a patch of darkness breaks away from the silhouette of the large tree at his back and descends silently towards him.

45

'Stop or I shoot.'

She stops but it is too late. Watson is already dead, face down in the dried leaves.

Messi, who has made his way round the left of the rocky overhang and is now standing at the top of it, keeps the gun pointed at Gutner's chest.

'Step away from the body and turn around. Good. We are going to make our way back down the mountain to the cove. You are going to walk ahead of me. If you make any attempt to escape I will shoot. You will not attempt to remove your knife from the body. Is that understood?'

Gutner nods. Messi makes his way down the slope towards her.

'Now move.'

Gutner is limping, which will limit her ability to escape. Passing Watson's body, Messi thinks briefly of the occasion he met his wife and daughter, at a restaurant in Palermo. A sunny afternoon last October. Watson had too much to drink, as usual, and embarrassed everyone by making loud remarks about foreigners and their eating habits. Curious coming from an Englishman in Sicily who insists on eating cornflakes for breakfast and drinking only English tea. Who will be telling his wife and child that he is not returning home? Will they be sad or secretly relieved? Who will retrieve the body?

Eventually they reach the top of the narrow path that leads down into the cove. The pilot is standing on the shingle beside the helicopter, talking into his mobile. By the time Gutner and Messi have descended the narrow path, the pilot has finished his call.

'New orders. We are taking her to Corsica. Watson?'

'He won't be joining us,' Messi replies.

The pilot arches an eyebrow but offers no comment. A couple of minutes later they are in the air, heading west at one hundred and eighty kilometres an hour. Messi is on the front seat next to the pilot, as before, and Vikki Gutner is at the back, where Watson was lying. For the second time in one evening her hands are cuffed.

46

We have long since given up pretending that La Vita Nuova is doing anything other than slowly sinking, limping along but making steady progress. The dolphins are as concerned as we are and, when we slow to check that the calf is OK and that everyone is keeping up, it is Steve who tells Rafael to just keep going.

For some time Corsica has been growing in the west. Rafael says that the highest mountains on the island are over two thousand seven hundred metres. We are taking turns at the wheel. It is really tough going as the boat is listing badly and would prefer turning round and round in circles to making forward progress. When Rafa switches on the GPS for a few seconds and discovers that we are less than two kilometres from land we all give a massive cheer and do a pirate's hornpipe. At least that what I tell everyone they are doing when they copy me in a dance I saw some idiot do on YouTube.

Although we have drifted north, the storm is abating and it looks like we are going to make it. OK, what do I know?

A burst of whistles and clicks reminds me that we haven't spoken with the others for ten minutes or more. Leaving Rafa at the wheel I grab the hydrophone and laptop and go out on deck. Calypso leaps out of the water.

'Sam. I know where we are. This is my home sea. The place Steve and I were born. Everything is where I remember it. It's beautiful. I can hear the sea floor, the valleys and rocks. They are just as they were when I was a calf. When the light comes we will show you everything.'

She leaps again and, seeing her in the light spilling through the cabin window, I decide that this time her smile really is a smile. All four dolphins start to click excitedly and the translation software promptly gives up trying to make sense of anything.

The night air carries the faint smell of pine trees. Down the coast to our left, the lights of a small town that have been visible for a while have disappeared. I wonder if Rafa has spotted it. Maybe we should take our chances and change course. On the other hand it might make more sense to drop anchor some distance away and arrive on the island unseen. The worst option is the one we are committed to; we are heading straight towards a rocky promontory. We need to find a beach, somewhere safe to disembark.

I start making a mental list of what we will take from the boat, before it sinks, then notice a new noise. There is no sign of activity, no moving lights or anything else straight ahead.

'Rafa, grab the wheel a minute.'

I step outside. Back behind us to the east the story is very different. There is the faintest whisper of light on the horizon but instead of feeling relief that the night is finally coming to an end I feel a rising surge of fear. Low down, licking the sea, is a single light, pointing straight at us, and although I cannot actually be certain, I just know that it's growing.

Every time we think we have slipped the net we have simply passed into a bigger net.

47

Vikki Gutner has been doing a great deal of thinking as the helicopter speeds across the surging sea towards Corsica. That she is alive, and handcuffed yet again, means only one thing, she must still have information that is of value to someone. While Messi and Watson have never been allies, except in their mutual desire to ensure that a woman should not achieve a position of authority within 3-TEC, Messi would surely have shot her up on the hill if his authority included it. For the moment he appears to have forgotten she exists, having told her that they will sort everything out later if she behaves herself.

There has been no conversation as to why they are flying towards Corsica but the variables are clear; either Michel Blanchard has been discovered there or the boat carrying the children is heading in that direction. And, depending on the boat's speed, La Vita Nuova has either already arrived and docked or they are about to.

Although the completion of her mission is still on her to do list, it is no longer of primary interest; Survival and revenge have replaced duty. Tenebris has betrayed her. What is so important about these youngsters and the two dolphins? What did the young girl say, something about them talking? What does that mean? Is it true? Is that the real motivation for killing them all?

Messi speaks but Gutner cannot make out what he is saying above the roar of the engine. She leans forwards. Between the seats she has a reasonable view of the visual display for the thermal imaging camera. In a sea of black is a glowing dot of colour, a rainbow that goes from purple to orange to yellow and white. The dot is growing quickly as the camera zooms in, revealing that the dot has a pointed end and a blunter end. A boat.

On the wall behind her is a rack from which are hanging five sets of headphones. Gutner stands up, takes a set of headphones in her cuffed hands and pushes them over her ears. The headphone sockets are mounted into the sides of the headrests.

'Possible target at two o'clock,' Messi is telling the pilot. 'We need to pass over to confirm the target before taking it out. I need visual confirmation.'

'Understood.'

'We need visual identification of the occupants. Two teenagers and two children.'

The helicopter drops rapidly until it is thirty metres above the waves and closing on the target. If the vessel is a Corsican fishing boat, Gutner concludes, she will be safe but if they have found the youngsters it may only be a few seconds before she becomes surplus to requirements.

The gap closes rapidly. Five hundred metres, four, three, two … About forty metres from the boat the helicopter slows then hovers.

'I'm seeing two, three figures.' Messi peers at the thermal imaging display. 'Through the cabin window. We need a fourth.'

'I'll do a fly round.' The pilot leans across and presses the record button on the top of the thermal imaging display. A red dot illuminates top right of the screen. He flips the night vision goggles down on his visor and his view of the scene below changes dramatically.

Behind the pilot, Gutner sees that the boat is listing badly. It is definitely the right boat. The helicopter is now only twenty metres above the waves and circling in a clockwise arc.

A loud metallic ping, followed by another.

'There. Look. Shooting at us!' Messi shouts.

The third shot strikes the windscreen leaving a starburst crack in the bullet-proof glass. Messi flicks between the display modes to change the spectrum. Suddenly he has what he wants; a girl's face peering up from behind a crate. Sam Blanchard.

'OK, we have ID. Take them out.'

'Missile launch in five, four, three, two ...'

As the pilot speaks his night vision goggles are slammed back into his eyes and he feels a huge pressure on his throat.

'Bank right now. DO IT!' Gutner hisses, pulling the link between the handcuffs hard against the pilot's Adam's apple.

Messi is fumbling for his gun when the missile fires. A short loud hollow hiss followed by a streak of flame searing the air, the missile misses the boat by a couple of metres. It hits the cliff, some seventy metres away, creating a fireball that lit the sky briefly. A section of the cliff detaches and falls into the sea.

Messi has his gun out, pointing at Gutner's head.

'Shoot me and you have an eighty five percent chance of hitting the fuel line or the fuse box behind me,' she tells Messi. 'Do that and we are all dead. Feeling lucky?'

She is counting on Messi, who is an office man, not knowing that she is talking rubbish, and in the knowledge that the pilot is in no position to contradict her. For what feels like an eternity Messi keeps the gun pointing at her then, eventually, he lowers the barrel.

'Why, Gutner? What will this achieve?' he says.

'Listen carefully,' she says, ignoring his questions. 'We are going to fly to Bastia and touch down. Understood?'

She pulls hard on the handcuffs, the pilot splutters and groans.

'Understood?' she repeats.

Messi swallows and nods slowly.

'Now sweet talk him so he doesn't try anything stupid,' she adds.

48

'It's perfectly safe, Keisha. Just breathe normally through the mouthpiece, even when you're underwater. Rafa will be with you, shining a torch so it won't be completely dark and …'

'It's not that, it's something else.'

'The dolphins won't hurt you or …'

Keisha shakes her head.

'What then?' I shout, losing my patience with her. 'We've run out of time. We have to get off this boat now or we will all …

'I don't like fish,' she says quietly.

'What? WHAT? Dolphins aren't fish.'

'Any kind of fish. I can't stand them.'

'There aren't any fish.'

'In the sea there will be. I just can't.'

'What does that even mean, I don't like fish? How can …'

'They don't blink. They just stare at you with those eyes and they don't blink. I can't stand them.'

And she calls me a loopy fruit?

Let me explain. During the approach of the helicopter, we all panicked a bit.

OK, a lot. We panicked a lot.

Anyway we lost control of the boat, which drifted closer and closer to the cliffs before hitting a submerged rock, further damaging the already weakened hull. So now the boat is taking on water so quickly that we have less than ten minutes to abandon ship.

No, that's not right. We didn't all panic. The humans panicked. Calypso isn't worried, she is convinced that she has a way of saving us. Which is nice, even though I have pointed out to her that a helicopter is firing rockets at the boat, there are only cliffs ahead of us and, according to the GPS, the nearest beaches are seven hundred metres south or six hundred metres north.

'Put on your diving gear,' Calypso said. 'I have checked everything.'

So I went inside and explained the situation to Rafael and the children. Through the open doorway to the berths below we could all see a sleeping bag floating in the rising water.

'Houston, we have a problem,' Rafael said.

'Who's Houston?' Keisha asked.

'It's an old space thing. I'll tell you about it one day. Anyway, the problem is this: we only have diving kit for three. There are four of us.'

We all looked at each other.

'And I'm not sure that Fred or Keisha are big enough to carry your Dad's tanks or fit his mouthpiece in their mouths.

'We have to try,' I said from below deck, passing up his dry suit and mine. 'There's a five litre tank somewhere. I can wear Dad's kit.'

Neither Fred nor Keisha said anything while Rafael and I transferred the diving kit into the cabin.

'OK, you go with Keisha and Fred and I can wait until …'

'No, Rafa, let's draw straws,' I said. 'This has to be fair.'

I didn't say that we might all be about to die and that we had to randomise the risks. I didn't have to. We drew straws, first for Rafael and I, and then for Fred and Keisha. Steve and Calypso were calling, we had to hurry. Rafael picked the longer straw, then Keisha. They would go first. We carried the kit outside, which was when Keisha started her I don't like fish routine.

'Just take my hand and keep your eyes closed, and Calypso will pull us along. OK?' Rafael says, crouching down and holding Keisha's slender shoulders. 'You won't see anything, I promise.'

Keisha looks into Rafael's eyes then up at mine then back at his. 'Cross your heart and hope to die?'

'Cross my heart and hope to die.'

'I suppose …'

'That's great, Keisha. You're the bravest girl I've ever met,' Rafael says, drawing her to him and hugging her. He looks up at me and winks. 'Let's get everything ready.'

A minute later they are strapped up. Keisha looks tiny and fragile, burdened by the weight of the kit. Rafael climbs down the portable ladder into the sea and calls Keisha to follow him. Having made her mind up, Keisha shows only grim determination. I help her position herself at the top of the ladder. She climbs down and at the foot of it, hangs on while Rafael adjusts the regulator and helps her with her goggles. I pass him weights that he secures to her belt to counter the buoyancy of her scuba tank.

'Bite down on your mouthpiece. Like me.' He shows her. 'Yeah, like that. OK, arms around my neck and hold on tight.'

Keisha lets go of the ladder and wraps her arms around Rafael's neck. When she is relaxed enough to let go and bob in the water, Rafael secures the straps and clips that will prevent her floating away. There being no dry suit small enough for either Keisha or Fred, she is in her ordinary clothes and shaking with cold. As soon as he is satisfied she is calm and focused, Rafael takes Calypso's dorsal fin and nods. All three disappear underwater. I hope Calypso knows what she is doing.

'Come on,' I sign to Fred. 'We have work to do.'

We go back inside.

Rafael has found four submersible dry bags. He has stuffed everything he wants to save from the boat in two bags: the GPS, his passport and wallet, the gun, a spare t-shirt, Dad's laptops and various chargers. The iPad is sealed in its own bag and out on deck. I climb into my dry suit then go down to the sleeping area and wade about in the freezing water pursued by the floating sleeping bag, grabbing a change of clothes for me and checking that we aren't about to forget anything really important. I find Fred in the galley, stacking up plates and cutlery, the tin of hot chocolate, cups for everyone, bread, butter, jam and cheese, olive oil, tomatoes, and two large bottles of fresh water.

'We can't take all this,' I explain, pushing all the cups and plates away. Only the stuff we really need.'

Down into the hold, I sort through the diving equipment: two knives, Dad's diving computer, which I strap to my wrist, the medical kit, three torches, and every battery left in the box. I spot the small rollup solar panel charger and take it. Behind me the engine is beginning to splutter.

As I climb the steps back up into the cabin, the boat creaks and tips further to starboard. The piles of stuff we have collected slide across the floor. I check my watch eight minutes. Where are they?

I do a further quick triage of what we can take with us then ask Fred to cram everything into the bags as tightly as he can. I see that he has stuffed his fantasy book into one of the bags. He looks at me defiantly, daring me to say something. It's not worth fighting about. Remembering the mafia maps that show the fishing nets locations and the papers we took from Gutner's helicopter I pull them out of the cupboard by the wheel and cram them into my dry suit before zipping myself back up.

We have one bag for food and water. Fred sits on the bags to push all the air out while I zip them tight. Four bags containing all our worldly goods. We thread straps through them to link them together and drag them out on deck. The darkness of the night is slowly giving way to the first light of dawn. A couple of shrieking seagulls appear, skimming our heads before dropping down to glide over the surface of the waves. Fred disappears back inside the cabin, emerging seconds later with the small leather backpack.

Where are your brains, Sam?

I re-open the food bag and remove half the food and one of the water bottles. In their place I place the dragonfly drone, in its box, the remote controller, and the two memory sticks. We don't even know what is on the memory sticks yet, I realise.

'Just eat whatever you want to eat now,' I tell Fred. 'The rest we leave.'

I zip the bag and hug Fred as he stuffs a cake in his mouth. What would Dad would be saying right now, if he were here? How would he try to keep us all calm in the face of danger?

Fred pulls away and points at the sea. Steve and Calypso have reappeared. Steve is carrying one of the scuba kits; harness, the five-litre tank, mouth-piece and straps hanging from his mouth like an ugly octopus.

'OK?' I sign.

Calypso nods. 'They are safe. I remember everything.'

I pull the hydrophone out of the water and secure it to the iPad in its waterproof pouch. I check my scuba kit and, with a little help from Fred, haul it up onto my back. Everything fastened and the iPad secured to my belt, I plug in my earphones, cross over to the ladder and climb halfway down, taking the second scuba kit from Steve. The boat judders and drops in the water. I remove the weights from the belt and, with Fred's help, hang them over the gunwale. The scuba tanks and harness I leave floating on the waves.

A stream of whistles and clicks. The iPad screen is active.

'Pass me the bags,' Steve is saying.

He takes the string of bags in his mouth and dives. Seconds later he reap-pears on the surface, dragged up by the buoyancy of the bags. He dives a second time and again the same thing happens. There is too much residual air in the bags, we have to start again from scratch. I shout rude words at the night sky, thankful that Fred cannot hear what I am saying.

It turns out that he can also lip read the profile of a face.

'I'm telling Mum and Dad what you just said,' he signs, his face a picture of shock and horror.

Yeah, OK, I'm childish. I stuck my tongue out. My bad.

Steve is clicking loudly. We have to haul the bags back on deck and start again. What should we abandon? I am struggling with the options when two heads appear next to Steve's, the female and the calf. We watch in amazement as the female grabs one of the bags in her mouth. Together the three dolphins dive. We wait but bags and dolphins are gone. Fred pumps his fist in triumph.

'Hurry,' I sign, stepping off into the sea.

Fred comes down the ladder, dips a foot in the water, and hesitates. The water is freezing. I can almost see his brain working; Keisha did it and so will he. He clenches his teeth and jumps, gasping and thrashing about wildly in the cold water, as you do. I quickly strap him in to the scuba kit harness, secure weights to his belt, clip his belt to mine, open the valves on his tanks, and show him how to bite down on the mouthpiece.

'Can you breathe?' I sign.

Fred gives me a thumbs up. I fit his goggles and pull the straps tight, while Calypso waits patiently.

'Are you ready?'

Fred points behind me. I spun round. In the distance a headlight has appeared over the cliff top. The helicopter is back.

'Time to go,' I sign, grabbing Calypso's dorsal fin with one hand while pushing my arm through Fred's shoulder strap and holding on to his belt with all my strength. Calypso's head disappears beneath the waves and we are sucked under in a confusion of bubbles and noise.

49

'She's hardly moved,' the pilot observes. 'Down there.'

The helicopter descends rapidly towards the sea. Messi shifts the thermal camera's viewpoint and quickly locates the boat. She is listing more than she was ten minutes earlier. The sensors show the engine is still hot. There is no tell tale signature of the four occupants glowing against the dark blue background, but since they are approaching from directly behind the vessel, Messi isn't hugely surprised.

They have lost ten minutes thanks to Gutner who, with the links between her handcuffs pressing hard against the pilot's windpipe, directed them to land on the outskirts of the nearest town. As the aircraft's skid brushed the ground she released the pilot from the throat lock, slid open the door of the helicopter, and threw herself out onto the ground, in one fluid movement, rolling rapidly to her left, out of shot. Still handcuffed, she picked herself up and ran off zigzagging from side to side while the pilot was still struggling for air. Messi shouted at the pilot to chase her so that he might kill her there and then, but the pilot persuaded him that the boat was their priority; returning to the sea had to come first.

Approaching the listing boat, Messi acknowledges that the pilot was right.

'Do you want to investigate?' the pilot asks, slowing the helicopter.

'No. Blast her out of the water.'

The pilot lowers his night vision goggles into place and positions the cross hairs over the target.

'Missile launch in five, four, three, two, one.'

A second missile hollow-hisses from the launch tube. This time there is nothing to deviate the missile's path and it slams into the wooden cabin. The cabin disappears in a fireball, with splintered wood thrown high into the night sky. Beneath the fireball the boat falls apart like a collapsing house of cards. Once they have checked for survivors and satisfied themselves that no incriminating evidence is being left for others to find, they will deal with Gutner and contact headquarters.

50

It is exhilarating. It is terrifying. Clinging to Calypso, we are thrown this way and that as we hurtle through the gloom of a pre-dawn sea. All at once a massive rock wall looms out at us and, before I can even flinch at the thought of impact, we pass into the rock itself through a hole barely larger than a doorway. An archway? A fissure between the rocks of the cliff?

We are in absolute darkness. Buffeted by unseen currents, the scuba tanks on my back scrape loudly against hard surfaces, jarring my neck. Then it is my flippers and knees crashing against rough surfaces, twisting my legs, throwing my body away from Calypso's, threatening to loosen my grip on her dorsal fin. I sense we are traveling in a narrow column of water in which a torrent of dolphin clicks ricochet back and forth like the bubbles swarming in a boiling kettle. Dizzy and disorientated, I am desperate for the journey to come to an end, but it goes on and on.

Pulled right, then left, then up again even faster than before, painful pressure building in my ears. In the darkness Fred's hand grips tightly.

Another abrupt change of speed and I lose my grip of Calypso's dorsal fin. Her flukes beat once against my thighs and she is gone. My head bangs against rock. With my free hand I reach down for the torch. It is gone; Calypso's flukes must have torn the strap..

In front of me in the darkness my hand finds only water. I reach out to my left. Nothing. I could be floating in space. To my right, passing my left hand over the top of Fred's head, I reach solid rock, rough and lumpy. Is Fred all right? Where is Calypso?

Maybe I can locate my torch with my feet. I reach down with my foot, and find a gentle resistance like sand but softer and yielding. It feels as if as if something is grasping me in the darkness, cold sticky fingers wrapping around my ankles, pulling me down, like a spider rolling a paralysed fly in silk.

I kick my legs violently until the unseen tendrils release their grip.

Forget the torch, Sam.

Behind me my hand finds only water. Where are we? The rasping sound of my breathing, the liquid bubbles noises, Fred's hand gripping mine so tightly my fingers are aching, and the soft surface loitering beneath my feet, are my only link with reality. Should we fumble our way back, hand over hand, to find the sea? How far have we come?

Think, Sam, think.

Something bumps into my belly. I recoil in terror, lashing out, but my fists find only water. Has something risen up out of the quick sand or the mud at my feet? How big is it?

The knife. Grab your knife.

I will have to let go of Fred to reach my knife, the sheath is on the outside of my right calf. I loosen me grip on his hand and immediately I feel Fred grip more tightly, squeezing my hand so hard that the bones grind against and over each other. As I twist my body round to reach the knife with my left hand I am nudged again in the ribs this time. I pull Fred closer to me in the blackness. Why doesn't whatever it is simply bite off our heads and be done with it?

Another nudge. And a noise. Nudge. A burst of clicks. Nudge.

Finally I understand. I cautiously reach out my hand to find a familiar shape, smooth and yielding like rubber. I push myself away from the rock to Fred's right, taking Fred with me, to let Calypso pass. Moments later she is back, having turned around somewhere in the darkness. Her flipper brushes me and her back slowly slides along my hip. I grip her dorsal fin and she moves off. As I am pulled forwards my flippers catch again in the silt or mud, dragging my feet back before releasing me. We are on the move again, left and right, up and up until all at once it is over and the pulling stops and I am floating, my head no longer in water but in air.

No clouds, no stars.

I hear a voice, Rafael's voice but sounding weird. Water trickling sounds but different. Where are we?

'Sam. Sam.' Rafael and Calypso both calling my name. Calypso using that strange voice she used earlier, even stranger now as it echoes repeatedly in the darkness.

All at once there is light. Rafael's face is above mine, peering down from a funny angle.

'Are you OK?'

‘I don’t know,’ I answer, having spat out my mouthpiece. ‘Are you upside down?’

‘Turn around.’

I turn in the water, dragging Fred round with me. Rafael’s head is now in front of me, and the right way up. He holds a torch, pointed downwards and away from our eyes. Calypso is beside me.

‘Where are we?’ I ask.

‘We need to ask Calypso. Over here is much shallower.’

I swim forwards, quickly finding solid rock beneath my feet. We wade up and out of the water, where I remove Fred’s goggles and mouthpiece then push the hair out of his eyes.

‘Wow!’ he signs, eyes wide.

The pool of water is maybe four metres across. All four dolphins are in the deeper water where the pool disappears beneath a sloping wall of yellow, white, and orange rock. Floating beside the dolphins are the bags Fred and I packed. The light spilling from Rafael’s torch bounces off the water to create dancing zigzag lines on the rock above our heads.

We are in a cave.

A few metres from the far edge of the pool are a series of tall ghostly figures floating in the air, staring down at us. I draw a sharp breath then, as I remove my goggles, realise they are clusters of huge stalactites, white and translucent, the light on their blotchy glistening surfaces shifting with the light reflected off the water, creating the impression of motion. The dolphin calf is in a state of high excitement, squeaking and squealing as it looks at us, then at the other dolphins, then at the roof of the cave. Just like a small child.

‘Where’s Keisha?’ I ask in a sudden panic.

‘It’s OK,’ Rafael smiles. ‘She’s over there.’

The cave is huge, maybe thirty metres across. I cannot even see how deep it is. No wonder it sounds like an empty swimming pool. In places the roof dips down to two meters or less above the floor, at other points it vanishes up into the darkness. The air is cool but warmer than out on the sea.

Keisha sits quietly some ten metres away, her back against the cave wall, her face lit up by the mobile phone screen she is peering at. Fred has crossed the cave and now squats down beside her. From his trouser pocket he produces a plastic bag that he unties carefully. He offers her a handful of biscuits. Her face lights up. For a second it seems she is about to kiss him. Fred leans back and the moment is avoided.

'I'm letting her play some game on my mobile,' Rafael explains. 'She was completely freaked out when we arrived. It's calmed her down. Let's get the other stuff out of the water.'

'What happens when your battery dies?'

'I know. I'll take it off her in a minute.'

I turn back to the pool, unclip the hydrophone and iPad from my belt and place the hydrophone in the water before wading across to collect the floating bags. The dolphins click and whistle animatedly, their noise lost in a soup of echoes and reverberations bouncing off the cave walls. I hope against hope that I have properly sealed everything.

Steve disappears, leaving Calypso, the other female and the calf waiting patiently while we open each bag in turn, checking the contents before moving on the next one.

'There's a dry t-shirt for you both,' I call out to Keisha. 'You need to get dry.' My voice echoes back and forth. 'get dry … get dry …'

'Is this all the food and water?' Rafael asks.

'Don't even start,' I warn him.

Calypso speaks. As I turn to the tablet for a translation, she repeats herself.

'OK, OK, give me a second,' I sign then pick up the tablet. We are looking each other in the eye when the same pattern of squeaks and squeals occurs a third time. We both turn.

The calf has her head above water and is looking directly at me. Even in the echo chamber of the cave it is clear where the sound is originating; the calf is mimicking Calypso. And, looking at the tablet, the phrase is clear enough for the translation software to have understood it.

'I'm taking the calf to safety then I return. I'm taking the calf to safety. I'm taking the calf to safety.'

'We need to find the other exit.' Rafael says over my shoulder.

'What do you mean?'

'To get out of this cave.'

'You're not saying that this is the only way out?' I point down at the pool.

'No idea. We were waiting for you.'

We are both thinking the same thing. When Calypso told us she knew a safe hiding place we didn't ask any questions. Now we are in the middle of a cliff, cut off from the rest of the world. If the only access is via a long underwater tunnel, we are now totally dependent on the dolphins for our survival.

And we can forget getting a phone signal.

Hearing a rippling of water behind us, we both turn in time to see three sets of flukes sink beneath the surface of the pool.

51

I am doing OK until I turn the corner and can no longer see the main cave. Darkness is loitering malevolently at the edge of the torch beam, a thick blackness so complete and so powerful that it can rip the heart out of my weedy light if it chooses and plunge me into a dizzying horror.

It is a cumulative thing. In a few hours I have dived three times into the midnight sea near the fish pens. I have seen a corpse drop in front of me and watched a tiny purple fish swimming out of a dead man's mouth, and I have become lost with Fred in the black tunnel that brought us from the open sea into this ancient labyrinth. It is too much. My nerves are shot.

I try focusing on the beauty of the scene, the cave walls swirling around me like petrified water, the stone smoothed by millions of years of erosion as an underground river has eaten the rock's rough edges into rounded contours that snake from the heart of Corsica down to the sea.

I press on, hoping the passage will end in daylight and fresh air. As in the main cave, the range of colours is amazing; oranges, yellows, sandy browns and ochres. In places large blotches of white rock form a translucent glistening skin over darker surfaces. Elsewhere the walls carry strange black marks. Without my noticing, the roof of the cave has slowly dropped down until it is almost brushing the top of my head.

My foot kicks something hard that spins across the floor and smashes against the rock ahead of me. I yelp, from the shock as much as the pain. Flashing the torch beam, I see a huge skull with three empty eye sockets and two huge flesh-ripping teeth leering up at me. I throw myself against the wall.

Calm down, Sam.

A second, more careful, look at the skull, while I rub the back of my head, reveals that one of the three 'eye sockets' might once have housed a nose.

A lion? A bear? Does Corsica have large predators?

'Sam … Sam … Sam … Sam …' Bouncing off the rock, Keisha's distant voice echoes around my head.

I am not sad to leave, retracing my steps, walking backwards and keeping the torch beam fixed on the skull until I have turned the corner. I turn heel and run back to the main cave. Behind me the darkness regroups, like raindrops finding each other on a windowpane, and watches me run away.

I hear Rafael coughing before I see him.

'Any luck?' he asks, emerging from another tunnel as I arrive in the main cave.

'Nothing. A huge skull. Nothing.'

'A fossil?'

'I'm David Attenborough, right?' I snap. 'Sorry. Stressed out.'

'Where I was, there is a thin current of colder fresher air coming from a side passage.'

'Air coming from outside?'

'Don't know for sure but, yes, maybe.'

'We have to contact my Dad in less than forty five minutes.'

'We have two choices, find another exit or go back down the tunnel to the sea.' Rafael can see from my face what I think of the second option. 'I'll go,' he volunteers, 'if you trust me.'

'Don't be stupid, Rafa, of course I trust you. We've survived this far together but look at you. Coughing fits, asthma and laryngo … whatever.'

'Laryngospasm.'

'That.'

He smiles. 'I'm OK. Let's set everything up by the pool.'

Reaching Fred and Keisha we find them both in dry t-shirts, several sizes too large for them. One of mine and one of Rafael's

'We've spread clothes over there to dry,' Fred explains.

'There's fifteen biscuits, one bottle of water and some olives and cheese,' Keisha announces. 'And I found this.' She hands Rafael his inhaler.

'All the electronic stuff is there. There's one more torch with a winder, the two head torches have batteries. All the bags stayed dry.'

I hug them both, as pesky kids go they are doing OK.

'We'll use these,' I say, winding my torch up again, 'in case we need the batteries for Rafael's mobile phone.'

'You're soft. There not the same batteries, are they?' Keisha says. 'Are we safe now?'

‘I hope so,’ I answer truthfully, wringing out the wet tops she and Fred have placed on stalagmites. ‘We’ll eat and rest for a few hours then we need to get out of the cave and contact my dad again.’

‘This place is too dark and scary.’

‘Calypso and Steve are back,’ Rafael calls out.

I join him by the pool.

‘Where are the other two?’ I sign.

‘The pod are one breath from here,’ Steve answers. ‘They are safe.’

‘Everyone is sad for the dolphins that died,’ Calypso adds. ‘Ten members of the pod were killed by the fishermen a few days ago.’

‘I’m sorry, Calypso. We’ll find a way to stop this.’

Easy words. We stand in silence, each of us thinking how powerless we are. Without thinking, I wade into the pool and sit down beside Calypso and Steve, taking the iPad with me. Rafael follows me.

‘How do you know this place?’ I ask, as Fred and Keisha join us in the pool, in spite of the cold. Keisha reads Calypso’s words on the iPad. Unselfconsciously, she hugs each of the dolphins in turn and I realise in that moment that we really are becoming a pod.

‘Don’t get that t-shirt all wet,’ I tell her.

‘I know.’

‘We played here when I was small,’ Calypso says. ‘We were brought here by one of the mothers to help us develop our echolocation skills. The pod has brought young dolphins here for a very long time. It is always dark. Like you, I am seeing the cave with my eyes for the first time. We liked the noises the cave made. We played in here for hours.

‘It must be dangerous.’

‘At that end of the pool are the bones of one of my brothers. He hurt himself on the way in when I was young and we couldn’t help him. After that we stopped coming.

‘We must be the first humans to ever set foot in here,’ Rafael says.

‘What? The first people ever? Keisha asks in amazement. ‘In the whole world?’

There is a tug on my sleeve.

‘We are not the only people in here,’ Fred signs.

‘That’s not funny,’ I say, alarmed. ‘Scaring people is stupid.’

‘It’s true,’ Fred insists. ‘I’ll show you.’

He takes my torch and shines the beam towards the far wall, beyond the pool. We all gasp, I swear, even Calypso's and Steve's blowholes hiss. Painted in black on the ochre surface is a line of horses running across the rock. Fred moves the torch to the left to reveal five white hands surrounded by black paint. One of the hands is much small than the others. A child's hand.

'These must be thousands and thousands of years old. Like those rock paintings in France and Spain,' I mutter.

'Move over Indiana Jones,' Rafael says quietly. 'Prehistoric discovery scenario.'

What is it with Rafael and all his endless scenarios?

Calypso and Steve are whistling and clicking beside us.

Fred shifts the beam again towards a group of huge stalagmites that have reached the floor to form thick columns.

'Oh wow, that's amazing,' Keisha grabs my hand. 'Look on those tall thin rocks. They're covered in jellyfish. Has someone painted them?'

I nod.

'How do they paint them in the dark? There's no elecky in here, do you know what I mean?'

'Maybe they did the paintings outside then carried the rocks in,' I suggest, keeping a straight face.

'Do I look that stupid?'

'Well, what do you expect, Keisha? They used candles, you donk.'

As Fred moves the torch beam he reveals that some of the jellyfish are painted and some are scratched into the rock. Where the stalactites meet the roof they are fronded with smaller stalactites that reach down like fingers. Even the rocks look like jellyfish. How have we missed the paintings earlier? Once you see them clearly you cannot not see them, they are so obvious.

'This is the biggest one,' Fred signs, shining his torch beam upwards at the roof to the side to the pool.

I don't think any of us can believe what we are seeing. I look at Rafael then at Calypso and Steve, then at Keisha and lastly at Fred, who is looking pretty smug.

'Dolphins and people have been friends for a long time, haven't they?' Fred signs.

52

The moment I lay eyes on it I know that the painting on the roof of the cave is one of the most amazing things that we will ever see and, judging from the silence, all the others sense it too.

Much of the roof of the cave is hairy with those tiny stalactites that hang like pale thumbs and fingers, but there are also patches of bare rock. The painting is on an expanse of rock about three metres above the floor. White and covered in scratch marks, like someone has dragged their fingertips across wet clay, this patch of rock is maybe three metres wide and two metres high. At one end are three human figures, drawn in outline and seen only from the waist up. Two male and one female. A line runs between their hands that are held out in front of them as if holding a handrail, or a piece of string. Below the figures are the outlines of two fish, scratched into the rock. The surface of the two fish is white and shiny, the only elements in the painting that are not covered in scratch marks. At the other end of the painting are three other forms. You cannot mistake them for anything other than what they are. Two are only partially visible, as if poking up above the waves, their dorsal fins and beaks clearly delineated. The last one is below the line held by the human figures and seen in its entirety.

We are looking at a prehistoric painting showing three humans holding a fishing net, and three dolphins.

'Are they catching the dolphins to eat them? Keisha asks.

'No, that's not it,' Rafael says quietly. 'I have seen a film of fishermen and dolphins in Brazil. The dolphins drive the fish towards the beach and signal to the fishermen when to cast their nets. The fishermen catch the fish that swim into the nets and the dolphins eat the fish that try to escape. These cave men aren't catching dolphins, they're working with them.'

I sign Rafael's words for Calypso and Steve.

We all feel the same thing; the weight of tens of thousands of years of history revealed in this painting that has remained hidden since the last ice age. We all stare at the proof of cooperation between our species, a relationship that goes back to a time when Europe was covered in trees and the seas were full of fish. A time before cars and laptops, trains and telescopes, churches and glass, clocks and wheels.

'There is another cave a bit like this one near Marseilles in France.' Rafael breaks the silence, his voice charged with emotion. 'The paintings there have been carbon-dated and between eighteen thousand and twenty seven thousand years old.'

'I have never heard of dolphins fishing with humans before,' Calypso says.

'We do it,' I say.

'We do many things that dolphins and humans have never done before.'

I find myself wondering what anyone would say if they found us at this moment, two dolphins and four humans sitting side by side in a pool of water admiring prehistoric art. Calypso has a point.

'I still don't like fish,' Keisha says, walking out of the pool. 'Scary eyes, even in paintings.'

She returns a moment later with Rafael's mobile phone and starts taking photos of the painting.

'Take photos of the other paintings too,' I suggest. 'And a photo of us all together.

'We already have,' Fred sign.

'What did he say?' Keisha asks.

'He said you are both little geniuses.'

I turn back to Calypso and Steve. 'We have to contact my dad in the next thirty minutes to let him know where we are. Unless we find another exit, one of us is going to have to go back through the tunnel and try to ring from the sea.'

'You cannot go back to the sea,' Steve says. 'There is a helicopter hovering above the waves. They have sunk the boat and they will kill you if they see you.'

He lifts his tail out of the water. In his left fluke is a round hole the size of a bullet.

'We will fetch you as soon as it is safe,' Steve says.

The two dolphins turn and disappear beneath the surface of the pool.

53

The passage is similar to the one I explored at the other side of the cave, but with a higher ceiling, some six metres or more above our heads. It is hard to see clearly, but it appears that high above us the twisting passage becomes wider, as if there is a hidden ledge close to the roof.

We have left Keisha and Fred in the main cave having decided, after ten minutes, that waiting and doing nothing is a recipe for disaster. A current of cold air brushes my cheek as I shine my head torch above us. Cleverly painted to fit into the contours of the rock are two lines of animals, a succession of horses on one side of the passage, and deer with huge antlers on the other. The floor rises slowly and eventually the ceiling is only three metres above our heads.

Turning a corner we find, to our dismay, that we have reached a dead end.

'That's weird. I can still feel the cold air.'

'Maybe there is something hidden above us on the ledge.'

'Do you want to climb up and take a look?'

Rafael holds his hands together in front of him. With the wall for support, I put my left foot on Rafael's hands and pull myself up. Right foot on his shoulder, I pull myself up a second time. Peering over the ledge the cold air current brushes my cheek.

'I can see a faint blue light,' I shout. 'There's a opening here.'

'I'll wait.'

'You'd better.'

I scramble up and crawl along the ledge on my hands and knees towards an opening.

'There's light at the end of the tunnel!'

'Is that a metaphor?'

'What?'

I enter the smaller tunnel, still on my hands and knees. The rock is wet and slippery. The light grows incrementally brighter until eventually, when I look up, I see a patch of grey sky above my head.

That is the good news. The bad news is that the gap in the solid rock above my head is only maybe thirty centimetres wide and twenty centimetres high. There is no way Rafael or I will ever squeeze through such a gap.

I climb down and we return to the main cave and explain to the children what we have found.

'Keisha can go with you,' Fred signs. 'I will stay here to tell the dolphins where you are.'

'No, We have to stick together,' Keisha insists, frightened for him.

'Are you sure?' I ask Fred.

'Give me three torches. You have to go and I am the only other person who can use sign language with Calypso and Steve.'

'What if something happens?' Keisha grabs Fred's arm.

Fred opens his mouth and screams to prove that, even if his ears don't work, his vocal chords are in working order. Ears ringing, Keisha, Rafael and I head back to the passage, past the animal paintings and on to the end where, after a bit of a scramble, we all make it up onto the ledge and along the damp tunnel.

'Remember, the phone must only be on for sixty seconds,' I tell Keisha for the sixth time. 'In the cave it doesn't matter because no-one can pick up the signal, but outside it's different. As soon as it is switched on you dial the number, don't wait for the address book to load. When you've told them we have arrived and listened to any message they have for us, switch the phone off and take the battery out.'

'I'll be waiting to catch you,' Rafael adds.

Keisha nods. 'What's out there?'

'I'll show you.' Rafael has brought the dragonfly drone with us. He takes Keisha's hand and places the drone on her open palm then, using the radio controller, he sends the drone up vertically towards the open air. We gather round the video display on the controller.

The camera set into the dragonfly's head rushes past the blur of rock and emerges into the early morning light. Straight ahead is a clump of bushes. Rafael turns the drone to the right to reveal trees in the middle distance. As the drone keeps turning, we see rock and, beyond that, more bushes and shrubs. The ground rises quite steeply. Further round again is more rock and then a road is revealed maybe ten metres away, dipping and disappearing at the bottom of the screen.

'OK?' Rafael asks.

Keisha shrugs her slender shoulders then nods.

Rafael brings the drone back down very gently until it is once again resting in the palm of Keisha's hand.

'Right, let's go.' I squat down. 'Put her on my shoulders and help me stand up.

Seconds later Keisha is squeezing up through the narrow hole. Her lime green trainers leave my shoulders and disappear into the fresh air.

I look at my watch and start counting.

54

'Who is this?'

'Keisha. Are you Sam's Dad?'

'No. I mean yes.'

'We are in Corsica. Is Sam's mum better?'

'What? Oh, yes. Yes, she is.'

'Did they take anyone else from the hotel to the ozzie?'

'What? Oh, you're the little girl who was in the garden, aren't you?'

'My dad was …'

'I'm sorry, Keisha, I cannot answer your question. Can you pass on a message to Sam and Rafael for me?'

'I suppose.'

'Someone important is flying to Corsica to meet you. They arrive very soon. Come to Bastia and ring in an hour. Bastia, you got that?'

'Bastia. We're a bit stuck, you know.'

'Ring in an hour.'

The screen reads call ended. It is cold and windy on the rock. High above her head, two seagulls fly over the empty road then dive out of sight beyond the rocks. Keisha can smell the salt. The sea must be down there, she decides.

She looks at the time; forty seconds. She should just have time to make another call, if she is quick.

About forty kilometres south of the rock on which Keisha stands, an Airbus A320 banks in the slate grey skies on its final approach to the small Aéroport de Bastia Poretta. The flight, which comes from Switzerland, has been held back in Geneva, due to delays to an incoming flight from Brussels, and took off twenty minutes late. Two small trees in front of the glass-fronted terminal building shake back and forth in the gusty wind. A small truck, shaped like a Labrador's head, pulls a snake of trolleys carrying luggage towards a second Airbus A320, bound for Venice. The truck driver steers with his left hand while stuffing his third croissant of the morning into his mouth with his right hand.

A large black Mercedes is waiting, engine running. The driver listens to the French football league results, waiting to hear how SC Bastia's opponents in the fight to avoid relegation have fared against Olympique de Marseille.

55

The Mustang jet slices the sky northwards, leaving a long white vapour trail in its wake. Sitting alone in a wide grey leather armchair, sipping his whisky and cocooned in the gentle hum that envelopes the main cabin, Tenebris knows that the next three or four hours will decide the outcome of the affair that has troubled him for several weeks.

Providing the services of specially trained dolphins to the military in war zones around the world is only one of the activities of 3-TEC but it is a service that has brought much kudos to the organisation over the past decade, And huge sums of money.

It suits the world's most powerful nations to outsource these services because it provides deniability. With so many do-gooders, non-governmental organisations, and animal rights activists keen to stop what they perceive to be the exploitation of intelligent creatures, it has become difficult for nation states to operate programmes that make use of dolphins, seals and other marine mammals to lay mines, protect borders, kill insurgents, and conduct surveillance. As importantly, the human talent to run these programmes is not found in one nation, but thinly spread around the globe. It makes sense to run private operations that can assemble the very best people, even if that means kidnapping them, in order to produce the perfect team, in an environment where those people will accept to work within the constraints provided.

Michel Blanchard has been one of the more difficult recruits, but eventually, like all the others, he was broken. His talent was obvious from the start. Properly managed, he has served 3-TEC well, earning the organisation many millions of euros, pounds, rials, dollars, dinars, riyals, and rubles.

Unfortunately, somewhere along the line, Blanchard has betrayed his keepers, subverted the programme and abused his position as chief dolphin trainer. His escape during military operations in the Libyan War has been embarrassing for 3-TEC and has resulted in a loss of trust, which is proving expensive, far more expensive than the loss of highly trained dolphins. When the previous attempt to recapture Blanchard failed some two weeks ago, and assuming that he might have survived the explosion on the Dauntless, Tenebris adopted a softly softly approach. Let the rabbit run and see where it goes. Who are his paymasters? Who will he turn to for support?

Two weeks later, Blanchard appears to have no friends and no plans, other than meandering up the coast of Italy in the company his daughter and the son of a minor mafia enforcer. No big conspiracy, just a loner on the run.

It has come as a surprise, therefore, that straight after sending Gutner to track them all down and kill them to bring the matter to a close, a phone call has changed everything. It appears that somehow one maverick loser has found another maverick loser.

The chance to settle an old score with Coemans, the man who cost Tenebris his left eye and left him for dead in the desert, is worth the inconvenience and expense of chartering a jet at short notice.

The door to the pilot's cabin opens and a thin blond man in a white suit crosses the sumptuous carpet towards him.

'The captain says that we are on schedule and due to land in twenty-five minutes. Would you like another drink, Sir?'

'No. Check my car and chauffeur are waiting. I have to leave quickly.'

'Of course, Sir.'

56

'What's she doing?'

'Maybe she's having trouble taking the battery out.'

'She doesn't have to do that outside. No-one can trace the phone once it's in the cave.'

''Well, I don't know. Tell her.'

'Keisha,' Rafael says then coughs. 'Have you finished?'

'Yeah, I'm coming.'

'What did he say?' I call up.

'Someone important is coming and we have to ring again in an hour, when we are in Bastia.'

'Who did you speak to?'

'Someone old and fat.'

Old and fat? How can you hear that someone sounds fat? Keisha has no idea what Dad sounds like, of course, or Sven for that matter since she has never spoken to either of them. I check my watch; nearly two and a half minutes since she climbed out of the cave and up onto the rock above our heads.

'Keisha,' I call.

A lime green trainer appears above us then another as Keisha sits down with her legs dangling over the hole. I feel a wave of relief.

'Drop the phone and I'll catch it,' Rafael says.

The phone falls into his open hands.

'OK, now lower yourself down and I'll catch you.'

Suddenly Keisha's legs and trainers disappear from view. She must be turning round.

Five seconds pass.

'Keisha, hurry up.' I call up. 'It's not safe.'

Silence.

'Keisha, don't muck about. Keisha?'

Rafael and I look at each other then up at the patch of grey sky. Rafael grabs me by the collar of my top and pulls me violently along the small tunnel, away from the hole and back towards the passage.

'Let me go. Let me go! We have to save her!' My voice is choked by the grip he has on my top.

We emerge from the six metre long tunnel and out onto the ledge over the passage that leads back to the main cave, Rafael hauling me round the corner and out along the ledge, as we hear a metallic ping, followed by a rolling sound. Now I understand. If the rolling sound continues we are as good as dead.

It stops after a couple of seconds, then starts again, then stops a second time. Rafael covers his ears with his hands and gestures for me to do the same. As I cover my ears I close my eyes but I still see the flash of light, through my eyelids. The thump of the explosion shakes me. Muffled through my hands I hear the smack of rock against rock.

I open my eyes and cough. The solid rock has protected us from the blast of the grenade; it cannot protect us from the cloud of dust

'We have to get away in case everything collapses,' Rafael says, switching on his torch.

We scramble a few metres further along the ledge overhanging the passage then, with Rafael holding my hands, I manoeuvre myself over the edge, my feet flaying about in the void until I find rock. I place a foot on each side of the narrow passage to brace myself then lean back to see how to get down. My feet are only a metre or so above the passage floor. Letting go of Rafael's hands, I land hard. The dust stings my eyes as Rafael's feet swing into view. I reach out and help his foot find a bump in the rock that will support his weight. A moment later he is down beside me. A plaintive scream echoes in our ears.

'Fred!' I gasp.

Negotiating a path between various shards of fallen stalactite, we race from the scene of the blast and back down the passage. As soon as Fred sees me he runs at full speed across the cave, dodging the stalactites and stalagmites. I can't remember when he last gave me a hug.

Rafael catches up with us. Behind him a cloud of dust is billowing into the main chamber.

'Where's Keisha?' Fred signs.

57

The in-coming flight from Geneva has landed and is taxiing along the runway towards the terminal. Four of the thirty-four passengers ignore the safety belt signs and the polite requests of the stewardess to remain seated; the same four passengers who delayed the flight earlier.

By the time the plane stops the three men and a woman are already by the door waiting for it to open. Bags in hand they run down the steps and across the tarmac to the black Mercedes. The driver takes their bags, except the briefcase held by the shorter of the two men, and puts the luggage in the boot while his passengers climb into the car.

The car pulls away from the parking space while the other passengers are still making their way down the steps. Pausing briefly at a barrier, the driver flashes a pass to the armed airport policeman. The barrier is raised and the car speeds away down the avenue of trees towards the main road that leads northwards to Bastia.

The man Tenebris knows as Pim Coemans has been very busy preparing for his breakfast meeting in Bastia's old harbour.

Michel Blanchard, his daughter and the Santoni boy face many enemies but few adversaries have as wide a reach as Tenebris, with his hidden contacts in armies, navies, mercenary organisations and governments around the globe. Coemans is under no illusions as to how much Tenebris wants to see him dead, indeed he is counting on that hatred being strong enough to undermine his adversary's legendary attention to detail. The very fact that Tenebris appears willing to come to Corsica shows that he is either supremely confident or unusually reckless.

From his vantage point on the fourth floor of a building across the old harbour from Bar Chez Jules, in front of the seventh century church of Saint-Jean Baptiste, Coemans surveys the comings and goings below through a pair of powerful binoculars. An hour ago two yachts left their moorings in front of the bar, to be replaced immediately by two rougher looking vessels.

Three cars vacated their parking spaces in front of the bar shortly afterwards. Twenty minutes ago, at eight fifteen, a van arrived to deliver four large parcels to the café. Since then all activity outside the building has stopped. The parking spaces in front of the café remain empty in spite of the traffic. The trap is set.

Coemans is sipping an espresso, with one eye on the old port and the other on the breakfast news on an ancient television in the corner of the room. Strangely, the news presenters are talking about the old port in Bastia and in particular about a large luxury boat moored in the middle of the harbour. Apparently the film star Wesley Bronson is in town, relaxing in Corsica for a few days before heading to Nice in southern France to complete filming his comedy thriller Nice Work 2. Coemans stands up and refocuses his binoculars and finds the boat. A member of the crew in an immaculately pressed white suit is carrying a large bouquet of flowers. On the television, the news presenters explain that Bronson is guest of honour at the Fête des Fleurs carnival that was about to take place in Nice. He will officially open the carnival the following afternoon. The presenters question whether or not the star is as popular as he was five years ago when the original Nice Work was released, while behind them footage from the first film shows the star falling into a pool while clutching a fat lady in a banana costume. Coemans is sure that he has once met Bronson and is trying to remember where and in what context when one of his mobile phones rings.

'Yes?'

'The plane has just landed. He has two people accompanying him. Dark Mercedes waiting close to runway.'

'Understood.' He cuts the call, rips the battery out of the phone and tosses another phone and the battery into the wastepaper basket.

'I know we have to hurry but we also need to eat and drink,' I insist.

Fred is looking at me with an expression that says, when did you turn into Mum? I know exactly what he means.

Rafael has been back to check if the passage roof has collapsed, to provide us an easier escape route, but we are not in luck and the underwater tunnel remains our only exit from the cave. By repacking everything carefully we manage to cut four submersible bags down to two. We are leaving what remains of the fresh water and food, leaving all the batteries and torches except the two underwater torches we need to complete the dive.

Fred puts his damp t-shirt back on and I stuff the one I lent him into a plastic bag with the mafia nautical charts that I then cram into my dry suit. No-one speaks. Now the decision has been taken, we focus on getting out of the cave as quickly as possible; we have to rescue Keisha, whatever it takes. We have to hope that the helicopter has gone and that it is safe to emerge into the sea but, to be honest, we are past caring, tired, battered, and desperate.

Fred is pushing something in my face.

'Are you even reading this? You can buy another copy when we get home.'

Fred sullenly stares me out until I take his paperback book and squeeze it into the plastic bag that contains the nautical charts. With all the stuff we have crammed into them, our dry suits have more lumps than badly made porridge. Rafael and I look like a couple of turtles.

One last look around at the incredible painting of humans and dolphins working together 18,000 years or more in the past and we are ready to leave our temporary home. As I wade into the pool, Rafael returns to the pile of our belongings and retrieves the gun we took from the helicopter woman.

'You never know,' he says, zipping it up his dry suit.

Fred is shivering as I tighten his straps, I wonder how long the tunnel to the sea actually is. On the way in we were in total darkness, pulled along by the dolphins. On the way out we will be diving down into the unknown. Fred is struggling with the scuba kit and, as I begin fastening weights to his belt, I instruct him to sit in the water to relieve the pressure on his shoulders. I fasten a strap to connect his belt to mine, long enough for us both to be able to swim independently. Fred's tank has air for no more than a ten-minute dive. I don't bother checking my own and I decide to say nothing; since we have no alternative means of escape it isn't worth worrying about.

Rafael clips the two submersible bags to his straps along with a third bag that he has filled with rocks to offset any buoyancy from the other bags. The iPad, in its sleeve, is clipped to his belt.

'Is Keisha still alive?' Fred signs, his big eyes staring hard.

'Of course she is,' I answer, pulling his goggles down into place. 'Remember how to bite on the mouthpiece?'

He nods.

The three of us exchange OK gestures, thumb and index finger making an 'O'. Rafael and I switch on our underwater torches and we wade to the deepest corner of the pool and sink beneath the surface.

Seven kilometres north of the airport, hidden in the bushes beside a derelict petrol station on the main road to Bastia, three armed men in combat jackets and headscarves stare southwards, waiting. One holds binoculars, the second holds a rifle with a powerful telescopic sight, and the third holds a mobile phone.

58

At ten minutes to nine the television weather bulletin, which is showing a mountain shrouded in cloud, is interrupted. Behind a nervous looking presenter is film footage of a large dark car in flames by a roadside, twisted metal, a long queue of traffic forming in the background, an ambulance and a couple of police cars in the foreground. The strapline at the bottom of the screen reads: À 3 kilometres de Bastia – un autre assassinat? A close up shows a Mercedes badge on the warped car bonnet.

Coemans leaps to his feet. Has someone killed Tenebris before he has even reached Bastia? Fluent in six languages including French, Coemans turns up the volume on the television and listens as the news presenter explains that the police have found a rocket launcher nearby. As yet no-one has claimed responsibility for the atrocity. The vehicle is believed to have been carrying a delegation from Brussels, an MEP, a government minister and two other officials, who all arrived at Poretta airport on a flight from Geneva a short time ago.

So not Tenebris, but still a catastrophe. Coemans is digesting the impact of the assassination on his plans when, at three minutes to nine, a large blue Mercedes arrives at the roundabout above the port and turns onto Rue de la Marine. Coemans at the open window, feels the breeze across his face and hears raised voices coming from a restaurant below, the repeated noise of an angry car horn, and the chopchop sound of a helicopter overhead.

The Mercedes, turns right on onto Quai Albert Gillio and pulls up outside Bar Chez Jules on the south side of the old port. The doors open and out steps Tenebris. He is not alone. Two thickset men in dark suits climb out of the other side of the vehicle. The three men cross the road and enter the bar as the car pulls away at speed.

From his vantage point above the port, Coemans sees the doors opening on the two boats that replaced the yachts in the harbour. Hidden from the view of anyone in the bar, six masked men holding rifles step out into the morning light. Pressed against the north side of the cabins they await orders.

With part of his plan lying in tatters in the twisted wreckage of a black Mercedes south of Bastia, Coemans focuses on the rest of the mission.

He is no fool. He knows his physical presence is distinctive and sees no need to put himself in danger if he can get others to do his dirty work. Having contacted the Corsican mafia with an anonymous tip off that the raid on mafia fishing nets off the coast of Montecristo was carried out by an organisation called 3-TEC, based in Sicily, Coemans has followed up with a second message providing the news that the organisation's head, a Major Tenebris, is meeting business associates at Bar Chez Jules in Bastia at nine am. That the Corsican mafia should then organise a welcoming party for Tenebris has been entirely predictable. All Coemans has to do is observe events from across the harbour. The second hand of his watch ticks slowly towards nine o'clock. In a couple of minutes Tenebris will be history.

But with ten seconds to go, the dark Mercedes suddenly reappears from the left and stops in front of the bar. As the car doors open, Coemans' heart sinks. Behind him the bells of the church of Saint-Jean Baptiste begin to toll.

59

Fred and I are following Rafael's flippers. If we hadn't already been through the tunnel, if we didn't know for sure that it leads to the sea, it would be easy to lose heart. The shape of the tunnel varies hugely, sometimes only a metre and a half in diameter, at other times three or four times that size. It's like swimming down a giant intestine, punctuated by the occasional stomach. Our torch beams cast wild shifting shadows along the walls and I am working hard on not imagining what lies in the many dark shadows and side passages.

The floor is thick with fine sand and sediment that blows up in huge clouds if we disturb it with our flippers. Having sunk into the sediment earlier, on our way in, I keep as close to the roof of the tunnel as I can. Every now and then a fish darts past, disappearing into the darkness ahead or behind.

At every junction we choose to go downward and hope we are making the right decision. I am trying to keep track of how far we have travelled, counting the metres as we swim. When I reach a hundred, the nerves start to jangle. When Rafael stops to check on Fred and me, he seems calm and relaxed. Rafael and Fred exchange a thumbs up.

Movement up ahead. Calypso and Steve arrive, whistling and clicking. I explain that Keisha has disappeared and we have to find her. We have to get out. Without a fuss, the dolphins turn and offer their dorsal fins. Rafael holds on to Calypso while Fred and I go either side of Steve. I keep my torch switched on. From what I can see, as we rush through the labyrinth of passages, we travel another hundred metres or so before a faint glow appears up ahead. Closer to the entrance, starfish and sea anemones cling to the walls. A huge lobster backs into a corner as we pass and, all at once, we pass through a thicket of kelp and out into the open sea.

The dolphins pull us along the seabed, banking right at speed. My dive computer, which has been on my wrist since we dived to rescue the dolphins back at the fish pens, tells me that we are thirty-five meters down. We pass over a large reef covered in red coral. An octopus appears out of nowhere, takes one look at us and vanishes downwards into a crevice. I draw Fred's attention to our boat, La Vita Nuova, resting in pieces on the seabed to our right. In a few months it really will be bringing new life again as fish, molluscs, sea urchins, and seaweeds colonise it and make it their home.

We are heading towards the surface. The sun has come out and the water is clear. Some distance away is a shoal of tall thin John Dory fish, their gleaming silver scales fracturing the sunlight and sending it in all directions, like those mirror balls over a dance floor. They turn to face us and, like sheets of paper viewed along their edges, disappear from view.

Two other dolphins, an adult and a calf, come into view, chasing a small group of red mullet. Beyond them the sea floor drops rapidly and there is only the blue of the sea. I wonder if they are the dolphins we rescued.

We surface some ten metres from a narrow and sheltered strip of beach, beyond which are thick bushes. I let go of Steve's fin as soon as my flippers touch the shingle then walk up and out of the water, pulling Fred until he too is able to find his feet. We sit on the sand for a couple of minutes, catching our breath and feeling the sun shining on our faces. The sea turns an intense beautiful turquoise in the brightening sunshine. Rafael lies in the shallows, tablet and hydrophone clipped to his dive kit.

'Thanks,' I sign. 'Your home sea is beautiful. The pink coral is amazing.'

'Did you see our calf?' Calypso asks. 'What happened to yours?'

It takes me a second to work out what she means. I explain what has happened to Keisha.

'We will return as soon as we can,' I finish. 'We have an important person to meet, Dad says. Then, if everything works out, we will all be safe.'

Neither Calypso nor Steve offers any comment on the idea that we might ever all be safe. I am not sure I believe it myself.

'Do people come to this beach?' Rafael asks.

It is a bit of a stupid question, given that neither Calypso nor Steve have set flipper in this stretch of sea for nine years.

'You want to hide something,' Steve observes.

'That's right.' Rafael leaves the hydrophone in the water, walks out of the water, removes his tanks and unzips his dry suit.

'Give us what you do not want to take. I will look after it,' Steve offers.

We hide the dry suits in the bushes with the scuba tanks and flippers. Having emptied the submersible bag that was full of rocks we retrieve various items from the other two bags and the stuff we carried in our dry suits and repack, keeping the one bag to take with us and handing the other two to Steve. Fred has put on my spare dry t-shirt but he is still shivering.

They need to be out of the water but safe,' Rafael explains.

'OK,' Steve says.

'Keep it safe,' Calypso says.

And this time when I say Calypso says, I mean it. She actually speaks. The sound comes from her blowhole, loud and squeaky, but recognisable English words.

Rafael, Fred and I look at each other then back at Calypso.

'How do you do that?' I sign.

'It is not easy,' Calypso says via the laptop. 'It is very tiring.'

'It's incredible,' I sign. 'Can you do it?' I ask Steve.

'No, Hurry and find the girl. We will wait.'

'Goodbye,' Calypso says through her blowhole.

We scramble up between the bushes and up onto rocks that led upwards away from the sea. There is no path but pretty soon we are standing by the side of a road. Ahead of us a tumble of rocks head upwards towards the mountains. Somewhere up above the road is the hole that Keisha climbed through. We rush up and down, shouting her name, looking for any sign that she might still be around, though Rafael and I know in our hearts that she has gone. Will the hole she climbed through even be visible after the explosion?

'We're in luck,' Rafael shouts. 'Look, a bus.'

A white single decker bus is coming towards us, heading south towards Bastia.

'Do we have any money?' I ask.

'Of course,' Rafael answers, holding a fistful of notes.

Fred is still searching frantically for signs of Keisha.

'She's not here, Fred. She'll be in Bastia by now which is where Dad said we must go. Come on.'

Fred isn't stupid. He understands that I can't possibly know where Keisha has been taken but he doesn't want to be left behind and, unhappily, he joins us by the roadside as the bus slows and stops.

60

We climb aboard. People stare as we walk up the aisle. Fred and I sit side by side while Rafael buys tickets. As Rafael reaches us and sits down, one row in front of us, the bus pulls away and the other passengers forget us.

On the other side of the aisle is a girl with dark hair, over-elaborate makeup and an orange coat. She looks to be about my age and is sitting with her mother.

'You know that dress Leila has? The one with the grey sleeves?' the girl says in French. 'It really doesn't suit her complexion.'

Yay, after weeks in Italian we are back in a language I understand and speak!

'You know what? She went out last week in that dress with a blue handbag. Can you believe it? Everyone was like she must be mad, or colour blind. I mean she might as well be holding a pink iPhone 4 with brown shoes.'

'Oui, Cherie,' her mum answers, her voice flat. 'Yes, dear.'

'Anyway, you promised me those hairclips and the hairband, the yellow one? I don't want the cheap one …'

It is like landing on a foreign planet. I try to imagine myself back at home. Have I been like that? As I watch the girl droning on, her mother barely listening, I cannot understand how anyone could be interested in such trivia. Doesn't she understand there is a real world on her doorstep? It is a month since I left home and in that time so much has happened that I can barely imagine being back at school, worrying about my hair, my homework, exchanging eyeliners on the way home. I have grown up.

'I don't want the ordinary one, it has to be a designer label, you know, something really classy and …'

'Can you please shut up before I have to tear my own ears off?' I say in French, leaning across the aisle.

As I lean back I see the mother's mouth break into a thin smile, which disappears as soon as her daughter turns towards her.

'Did you hear what she just said to me?'

The mother's expression is neutral, I guess she agrees with me.

Sitting in the window seat beside me, having seen that I am making a fuss and determined to pretend he has nothing to do with me, Fred is concentrating on warming up while staring at the passing landscape. It is a lose lose scenario, as Rafael would say if he weren't alternately coughing and snoring on the seat in front of us. As Fred's clothes dry out he is producing vast quantities of steam and is having to wipe the window clear every couple of minutes. He also smells quite strongly of seaweed and other stuff I've decided not to tell you about. It would reflect badly on the family. You understand.

The heat is getting to me too and I am struggling to keep my eyes open. I try to remember if the bus's destination sign said Bastia or whether it carries on after that.

Tenebris is sitting at a table towards the back of the café, close to the kitchen door and with a good view of the front door. The place looks clean enough, he likes the white tablecloths, clean linen inspires confidence.

One of his guards is sitting at a table in the window. Tenebris looks at his watch. Two minutes past nine. Coemans is late. He calls the guard over.

'Check Tony is OK at the back then do a sweep outside at the front.'

The guard disappears through the door to the kitchen. Tenebris turns to his unexpected guests.

'So, what did you say your name was?' he asks the smaller guest.

A mobile phone starts to ring. Tenebris reaches into the inside pocket of his sharkskin jacket.

'Someone has compromised our security,' Coemans's voice says in his ear. 'I should not have trusted you, the meeting is cancelled.'

The call ends.

Tenebris slips the phone back in his pocket as the guard emerges from the kitchen and walks towards the front of the café. Without saying a word, Tenebris stands and steps out of the room through the kitchen door. The door is still swinging shut when the large window at the front of the café implodes and the guard sinks to his knees.

One of Tenebris' guests turns to look towards the front of the restaurant. His thin moustache twitches involuntarily. The other guest has immediately dropped to the floor and is hurrying towards the bar area on her hands and knees, a pair of lime green trainers disappearing from view as the window of the front door is blown apart, showering the floor and tables with shards of glass.

Coemans races down the four flights of stairs and out into the street. He wants Tenebris dead but not at any price, not if it means killing children.

As he sprints along Rue de la Marine, around the old port, dodging the stunned tourists who are still trying to work out whether the noise that sounded like gunfire actually was gunfire, there is a second much louder bang. A ball of smoke and flame engulfs the helicopter that landed a short while ago in a car park at the sea end of Quai Albert Gillio, the road that runs the length of the southern side of the port. By the time Coemans reaches Quai Albert Gillio, the two boats that hid the six gunmen are already pulling away from their berths, heading between the rows of pretty white yachts and out towards the open sea. In the distance the twisted remains of the helicopter burns brightly.

Coemans runs into the café.

61

‘Terminus. Il faut descendre, Mademoiselle.’

I open my eyes and shake Fred as the little old lady smiles and walks off towards the front of the bus.

I rattle Rafael’s shoulder.

‘Where are we?’

We hurry off the bus. A huge sign tells us we are at the train station.

‘Now what?’

‘Now you ring my Dad and we all hope that his phone is switched on.’

Rafael produces his phone.

‘Not much charge.’

‘Just ring the number,’ I shout in frustration.

A tug on my sleeve.

‘Is Keisha here?’

‘I don’t know, Fred.’

Rafael has the phone pressed to his ear, waiting for the call to be answered. His face brightens.

‘Hello? Who is this?’

I snatch the phone from Rafael.

‘Dad?’

‘Sam. At last.’ It is Sven.

‘Where’s my Dad?’

‘As I told you before, he and your mother are safe. Now we have to worry about getting you to safety. Where are you?’

‘We’ve lost Keisha, the little girl. She was …’

‘I know about that. Are you in Bastia?’

‘At the station.’

‘Come to the old port. Take side streets and try not to draw attention to yourselves. It should take you just a few minutes then ring me again.’

Sven cuts the call.

‘Sorry, Rafa, I just wanted to …’

Rafael has gone. I spin round in total panic. Fred is still beside me.

'Where did he …'

'We'll need this.' Rafael races up behind me, clutching a map. He is wheezing and clutching his chest. 'I'll be OK. What's wrong?'

'Sven. He knew about Keisha. How could he? Whose side is he on?'

There is no sign of Tenebris. Standing in the backstreet behind Bar Chez Jules, Sven puts the phone back in his pocket and considers his options. It is unlikely that Tenebris will return, the odds are not in his favour. He will probably head back to the airport with the girl and wait.

Gun in hand, Sven pulls open the back gate to the café and makes his way along the alley between the dustbins to the kitchen door. The kitchen staff ignore him. If questioned later by the police they will no doubt say that they have seen nothing, assuming that the police do ask questions.

Sven pulls open the kitchen door and steps into the café. There is glass all over the floor and bullet holes in the walls. There are two bodies, a large man in a black suit lies face down on the floor by the front window, and a second man, with a Latin complexion and a thin moustache lies by a table at the back of the room. Although Sven has not seen Messi for a few years, he recognised him the moment he stepped from the black Mercedes minutes ago as the church bells were striking nine o'clock.

Sven reaches into the inside pocket of Messi's jacket. As he does so, Messi's eyes open and look up at him. He is barely breathing.

'Coemans,' Messi says slowly, blood gurgling in his throat.

Sven nods. 'Been a long time, hasn't it?'

'The girl …' Messi's eyes close and he stops breathing forever.

Sven stands up. The girl, what does he mean? What about the girl? Tenebris has abandoned Messi and the guard. But the girl is a bargaining chip, a hostage. He has taken her with him.

Sven goes back into the kitchen, it is safer leaving through the back of the building. A young woman is chopping potatoes with a heavy knife. A pan of water has started to boil. Sven pulls open the back door then hesitates on the threshold. What if he is wrong?

Back in the café, Sven looks around the room, trying to imagine what the gunmen saw. He crosses over to the bar and peers over the counter. Nothing except a few broken bottles, an upturned basket of croissants and pains au chocolat, a large fridge, the door of which is not quite shut, a dishwasher, and shelves stacked with crockery of various types.

“It’s Keisha, isn’t it?’ he says, tucking his gun into his belt. ‘You’re the girl I spoke with an hour ago.’

Nothing.

‘You know, Keisha, I don’t think you’re old enough to work behind a bar, or tall enough. What do they say in Liverpool? As much use as a bar of chocolate.’

‘Bar of soap, you miff git. As much use as a bar of soap,’ says a muffled voice.

The fridge door slowly opens.

‘You don’t know nothing.’ Keisha steps out of the fridge.

Sven puts his hands up in surrender. ‘I think we should get out of here before …’

‘… before the bizzies get here,’ she says, finishing his sentence. ‘Let’s go then, La.’

‘Sam, Rafael, and …’

‘Fred.’

‘… and Fred should be reaching the other end of the port in just a few minutes. Shall we?’ He offers her his hand.

‘I’m freezing. Do yer think they’ll give me a lend of a couple of those cakes?’

62

The streets all look the same, narrow lanes between four or five storey buildings painted in pastel shades, shutters on every window, cars crammed into every corner like teeth in a shark's mouth. It is a relief when we turn a corner and see the harbour beyond a car park at the end of short alley. Because Rafael's coughing fits are getting worse, I am carrying the submersible bag with the laptop, the iPad and all our other stuff. The strap is burning my shoulders. We pause at a bench to catch our breath. Rafael is keying Dad's phone number, or should I say Sven's number since he appears to have taken control of it, into his phone when Fred races away from us.

Heaving the kit back up onto my shoulder, I set off in pursuit then stop. Fred is slapping hands with Keisha, a high five, low five thing he copied off television. Keisha's heart isn't in it. Beside them is Sven, who smiles and, when I reach them, he thrusts his hand towards me. I consider it.

Why should I shake it?

'So where is this important person who is going to sort everything out?'

'You guys haven't …' Sven takes a deep breath, his hand drops to his side. 'There has been an assassination, south of Bastia, half an hour ago. The people I wanted you to meet …'

Why aren't I surprised? As Sven speaks, a ship's horn sounds. A large luxury motor yacht is moving slowly away from its moorings.

'… they were blown up in a car and ...' Sven turns to see what I am looking at. 'Wait here,' he shouts, sprinting away across the road and leaping over a low railing into the car park, a gun clattering to the ground in his wake.

'We had better pick that up,' I suggest.

In the distance a siren is sounding, then another and another. Trying to locate the source of the sirens, I notice the thick column of smoke about a kilometre away on the other side of the harbour. We hurry across the road. I pick up the gun and stuff it into the waistband of my jeans, and we continue across the car park. Sven is nowhere to be seen. A couple of rich old men dressed as sailors are eating their breakfast from yellow crockery on board a white yacht in the weak sunshine. Between them a vase holds a couple of pink roses. A woman with ridiculously tanned face and legs for the beginning of January walks along the nearest jetty carrying a wicker basket in which sits an ugly little dog with a huge green bow on its head while, in the opposite direction, two young guys are pushing a trolley packed high with polka dot patterned boxes and a palm tree.

We are very exposed in the middle of the car park on the edge of the harbour, surrounded by tall buildings. Two fire engines appear, racing down the right hand side of the harbour toward the smoke. A police car follows them.

'They blew up the helicopter,' Keisha says, her voice small and flat. 'There were loads of them with guns and that, and they blew up the windows of the café, and the man with moustache died, and the guy in the window as well.

'We should get out of here while we have the chance,' I say.

'What about Sven?' Rafael asks.

'What about Sven?'

'But your dad …'

I shake my head. 'We haven't spoken with my Dad, have we? We've spoken with Sven, who happens to have my Dad's phone. Sven says my parents are safe, and we believe him because we want to, but we haven't …'

'OK, great news …'

I spin round, gun in hand and point it straight at Sven.

'Prove to me that my parents are alive and safe.'

Sven looks at each of us in turn.

'Right now or I swear …'

'OK, let's all keep calm and …'

'Right. Now.'

'Sam, listen to me. I have persuaded the owner of that yacht to carry you all out of Bastia and on to France.'

'Four seconds, Sven. One … two …'

Sven looks round at the yacht then back at me.

'Why do you have to make things so difficult?'

'Three …'

Sven sighs and reaches for his pocket.

'Do that very slowly and very carefully,' I advise him.

He pulls a mobile from his pocket, keys in a number then passes the phone to me. A single long tone followed by silence then another long tone then silence then …

'Hello?'

''Dad!' I gasp.

'Sam. Where are you?'

'Should I trust Sven?'

'Yes.'

'How is Mum?'

A hesitation.

'She'll be OK. Fred …'

'He's here.'

'… and Calypso and Steve?'

'Yeah.'

'Trust Sven. For now.'

'OK.'

'Bye Sam. Love to Fred, and Rafael.'

I cut the call and realise I have already lowered the gun.

The yacht's horn sounds again.

'We have to hurry,' Sven says. 'Shall I take that?'

I give him his gun. We have another in the bag, if we need it.

63

The yacht is back in its berth. As soon as we have all climbed aboard, the gangplank is pulled in by the crew and the vessel begins moving sideways away from its mooring.

The two crewmen are in bell-bottomed white linen trousers and blue t-shirts. One is sporting an anchor tattoo on his right arm. Frankly, it looks more camp than macho.

'First, I will show you to your rooms then, when we get underway, I'll take you to meet Mr Bronson,' says the guy with the tattoo. 'I'm Tim. Shall I take your bag?'

'No, that's OK.'

We follow Tim through an open door and down two flights of steps carpeted in turquoise, as the boat taxies slowly between the dozens of boats moored in the old port, heading toward the open sea.

He stops at the second door.

'Cabin for the gentleman.' Looking at Sven.

Then, at the third door, 'and for the young couple.' He sees the look on Rafael's face and my own. 'For the young man,' Tim quickly corrects himself.

'The two children,' at the fourth door. 'And, finally, the young lady,' pointing at a fifth door.

'Good recovery,' I say.

Tim gives a brief smile then claps his hands daintily. 'Now listen carefully everyone. You have a little time to freshen up. Mr Bronson will meet you for lunch, which is at two o'clock. I will see what we have in the way of proper clothes. We are expecting to …'

Proper clothes?

Tim is interrupted by a coughing fit from Rafael.

'That sounds nasty,' Tim observes when Rafael has stopped. 'I'm sending the ship's doctor to have a look at you. Where was I? Yes. We are expecting to dock in Nice tomorrow morning, in time for the Fête des Fleurs, which is always absolutely gorgeous. Mr Bronson is guest of honour for the opening ceremony. Can you imagine! You can call me from your cabins if you need me for anything. Dial four six five.' He glances down at our feet and wrinkles his nose. 'Oh, you might like to take that footwear off before entering your cabins.'

Tim heads back towards the stairs.

'Fête des Fleurs is a flower festival,' I explain to the others. 'Excuse me, Tim,' I call after him.

He spins on his heel and stares back up the corridor.

'We have to stop, maybe fifteen kilometres up the coast. For five minutes, to collect some things and to say hi to a couple of friends. '

Tim gives a dramatic sigh, 'I'll see what I can do.' Another heel spin and off he flounces.

I join Fred and Keisha to check out their cabin. We remove our shoes, push open the door, and step inside. The lights come on automatically. Our jaws drop.

Money as an offensive weapon. Posh treehouse meets fabric shop.

All the fabric in the room is double to requirements. The bedcovers appear to have melted. Heavy swathes of pink fabric form pools on the floor at each corner of the huge double bed like puddled icing. The caramel-coloured curtains are gathered at the waist with thick gold ropes making plump bellies of cloth that bulge like a fat man's dressing gown, while more fabric trails sumptuously across the carpet.

Sprawled across the bed lie a dozen plump cushions, each edged with gold rope. Too weird even for Alice in Wonderland, four of the cushions have legs and feet made from huge gold pompom tassels at the end of a short length of gold rope. They look like sleeping ravioli dogs.

In order to ensure there is also twice as much carpeting as is strictly necessary, someone has decided that it looks really cool if the ceiling has the same flesh coloured carpet as the floor.

It is like being squashed into a ham sandwich.

To complete the look, the walls and all the furniture are in dark mahogany, the wood so thick with varnish that it looks like the wet-look gel that some of the boys at school wear to impress some of the girls. Like the cushions, every edge on every surface is trimmed with gold.

'It's amazing!'

'It's disgusting!'

Between them, Keisha and Fred sum it up quite well, in my opinion.

'The bathroom is here,' I say, gazing at a decadence of scallop-shaped bath and sink. 'Have a good wash before you touch anything.'

Keisha presses a button and triggers a mahogany roller blind to rise silently, revealing a huge display screen.

'Can we watch TV?' she signs.

'Bath then TV. See you later.'

I pull the door closed and find myself face to face with a large woman in a white uniform carrying a briefcase and wearing a stethoscope.

'I hear there is a nasty cough,' she says in a deep and resonant voice.

I point at Rafael's door.

'Marvellous,' the doctor says.

I check out my own cabin. To my relief I am spared the excesses of the other cabin, but at a cost. Mine is a temple to beige with a shiny disco floor ceiling. Think massive poached eggs with blue yolks floating on the surface of an orange pond and you have nailed the quilt cover design on the two single beds. There is a distinct smell of wood polish. The whole room is specially designed to make vomit less visible in a storm, I guess.

Calculating that it will take at least half an hour to travel up as far as the small beach where we left our dry suits, I take a quick shower then, bag in hand, it isn't leaving my side for a second, I knock on Rafael's door. No answer. I knock a second time then gently push the door. Rafael's cabin is almost identical to Fred and Keisha's, except the ham-coloured carpets are avocado coloured and the gold stuff is all silver. Rafael lies sprawled across the bed, fast asleep. Beside him is a strip of tablets, one tablet missing. The prescription says they are antibiotics.

I tiptoe out, pulling the door shut behind me and go upstairs to check that Tim has organised for the boat to stop further up the coast.

64

Major Tenebris sits in the back of the speeding taxi and considers his next move; not easy given the overpowering smell of cheap air-freshener and the acrid tobacco stink of the driver whose fat neck is dripping with sweat even in the cool of mid-January.

It seems most likely that, for all his accusations, Coemans is behind the mafia attack. It appears that three 3-TEC employees, Watson, Messi, and their pilot, are all dead. The whereabouts of Vikki Gutner are unknown, and Blanchard, his daughter, the Santoni boy, and the dolphins are all still at large. In the rush to escape the café Tenebris forgot to take the child, so he doesn't even have a hostage.

Should he head back to Sicily or run operations from Corsica? He cannot afford any more failures; on the other hand 3-TEC is about more than two dolphins, however remarkable.

They approach Poretta airport down an avenue of trees at the end of which is a roundabout and, beyond that, the terminal buildings.

'Straight to the security gate,' he advises the driver. 'The jet is two or three hundred metres down on the right.

They reach the barrier, where Tenebris winds down his window to show the guard his passport. The barrier lifts and the car sweeps through. Only as they reach the jet does Tenebris discover, parked on the far side of it and previously hidden from view, a helicopter. He turns his face away from the window.

'Drive past,' he orders the driver as he pulls his phone out of his pocket. 'Stop when we are out of sight of the helicopter.'

The call is answered.

'Jules, has Coemans showed up?

Tenebris has left his remaining guard at the old port with instructions to keep an eye on the comings and goings.

‘Very interesting news, Sir. I have just spoken with a couple of local fishermen who saw our targets enter the old port about twenty minutes ago, shortly after you left. I was at the other …’

‘Forget the excuses. Give me the facts.’

‘A young woman and a youth arrived with a boy. The fishermen noticed them because the young woman was tall and she was carrying a heavy bag while the youth carried nothing. A young black girl ran towards them accompanied by a tall heavily built man, large nose, moustache and hair pulled back off his face.

‘Coemans?’

‘Sounds like it.’

‘Go on.’

‘One fisherman thought they may have got on a large boat. Which would tally with what I saw from the other side of the port. A large luxury yacht, white with a blue hull, left the port heading north.’

‘OK. New topic. Why is a helicopter is parked next to my jet?’

‘Don’t know, but I would guess the pilot is Vikki Gutner.’

Tenebris ends the call. Gutner? He accesses the tracker app on his phone and sure enough, Gutner is at Poretta airport. Strange.

‘OK. Driver, you can park in front of my plane.’

The driver turns the taxi round and pulls up in front of the 3-TEC jet. Tenebris strides over to the helicopter and taps on the windscreen.

‘Let me guess, Vikki, you’ve bought a new helicopter with your own money to replace the one you destroyed?’

She is sitting stiffly and appears tired, bruised and less impeccably groomed than usual. Her flying jacket is torn. Tenebris pulls open the door.

‘Move along,’ he says.

Gutner points in front of her. The helicopter has only one cyclic, or joystick control, instead of the usual two; she has to sit where she is or Tenebris will have to pilot the aircraft. He walks round then, as he is about to climb in, remembers something. Gutner watches him cross over to the jet, the door of which opens downwards to reveal a set of steps. He climbs aboard and re-emerges moments later with two bags.

‘Right, a little job for you. Sad about Watson and Messi, don’t you think?’

Gutner who knows nothing of the destruction of the helicopter or of the death of Messi, arches an eyebrow. It might be to her advantage if Tenebris believes her responsible for both deaths.

'Absolutely tragic, Sir,' she says, firing up the engine. 'But then they were office boys out of their depth.'

'True. Our targets are heading north on a luxury yacht.'

'Our targets?'

'The Blanchard girl, Rafael Santoni, and others.'

'Their boat sank just off the coast about fifteen kilometres north of Bastia.' Gutner explains. 'The vessel had been involved in a collision and was taking water.'

'So I heard from Messi. And now our fugitives are on a larger boat in the company of a man who has long exceeded his sell by date.'

Gutner requests and receives clearance to leave. The helicopter rises rapidly in the sky before heading northwards at speed across the flat plain that lies between the sea on their right and the mountains on their left. Tenebris meanwhile opens his bags. The longer one contains an AW sniper rifle with a Schmidt and Bender PM II telescopic sight. Gutner knows the weapon well; she has used one extensively on the firing range.

The second bag contains half a dozen hand grenades. Tenebris puts the bag on the floor between him and Gutner but, in doing so, one grenade falls out and rolls under her feet.

'Can you pick that up?' he asks her, worried that it might wedge under her pedals.

'My back, Sir.'

In the circumstances, Tenebris decides not to lose his temper. He unfastens his safety belt, leans over and collects the grenade, noticing the dried blood on her trousers. He wonders how much of a fight there was between her, Watson and Messi.

Approaching Bastia, Tenebris briefly considers asking her to touch down near the old port so that they can pick up Jules then, seeing the burnt out hull of the other helicopter still smouldering at the harbour entrance, he changes his mind.

The town is quickly behind them.

‘The boat went down there,’ Gutner says, minutes later, pointing down towards the sea close to the cliffs. ‘I am surprised they survived. As you can see, getting ashore wouldn’t have been easy.’

Tenebris scans the shoreline as they continue northward and spots a narrow strip of beach. A pair of dolphins break the surface of the water, heading north. Could they be the ones? He toys briefly with the idea of spending a couple of minutes with the rifle but the lure of finally catching Coemans proves too great. First things first.

A minute later his eyes light up. Half a kilometre ahead is a large luxury yacht, white with a blue hull, stationary in the water.

‘OK, Gutner, this is your opportunity to redeem yourself. If all these targets are removed then the unfortunate incidents through the night are marked down as enemy fire.

‘Yes, Sir.’

Gutner tweaks the collective control and the helicopter’s speed slows right down until it is hovering. The instruments show their altitude to be around one hundred and fifty metres.

Tenebris removes the caps from the telescopic sight and surveys the boat. At last! On the lower aft deck, sitting at a table with a man in a white uniform, his hair longer, his face a little fatter, is Coemans.

Suddenly the boat disappears from view and the helicopter is moving again, heading west.

‘What are you doing?’ he shouts.

‘Better not to give them too much advance warning, Sir,’ Gutner replies as the helicopter passes over the cliffs and the yacht disappears from view. ‘We’ll approach out of sight then drop down close to the vessel. You’ll get more shots in that way.’

Tenebris nods, Gutner is shooting up in his estimation. It was an error sending Watson and Messi and he will have to make it up to her.

65

'This is a large yacht, Mademoiselle, not a dinghy.' Tim makes a sarcastic meal of the word Mademoiselle.

'You promised we would stop when I asked,' I remind him, controlling my urge to comment on his silly anchor tattoo.

'I said I would ask. And now we've stopped so what is the problem?'

'We've come too far, we have to go back.'

We are on the lower aft deck. Sven is sitting in the weak winter sunlight. On the table beside him is an espresso in a gold cup.

'Tell him,' I say to Sven.

Sven strokes his moustache. 'Maybe they saw us and will catch up.'

As he speaks I become aware of the sound of a helicopter. The experience of the past twenty hours puts me immediately on my guard.

Rocks and bushes flash past in a blur. Shortly before the edge of the cliff Gutner puts the aircraft into a hover. Tenebris opens his window.

'Let's hunt us a squirrel,' Tenebris says, something his father used to say when he was a child.

The helicopter moves over the cliff edge and out over the sea. The yacht is now only a hundred metres away and Tenebris can see Coemans clearly. He raises the rifle and puts the telescopic sight to his eye, panning the crosshairs across the waves, searching for the boat. He hears Gutner open her door, to make it easier for him to fire out of both sides of the aircraft if he needs to. Good thinking.

The thing with a carpeted floor is that you don't hear small things drop. What Tenebris does notice however is the way in which the helicopter starts to climb rapidly, throwing him forwards and causing him to lose his shot. He takes his eye away from the telescopic sight.

'Have we got a problem?'

Gutner appears to be struggling with the joystick.

‘These machines climb vertically at 12.5 metres per second,’ Gutner says calmly.

‘I can see that.’

In front of her on the instrument panel, the altitude indicator is whirling through the numbers.

‘Is the joystick stuck?’

‘It is called a cyclic, Sir. Another fourteen seconds at twelve point five metres per second and we will have reached …’

‘Don’t talk, do something. Use both hands.’

‘I am doing something. Do you know those dolphins can talk?’

‘Of course I do, that is why they have to die. Have you even begun to consider the repercussions for humanity if we acknowledge the existence of another sentient species on the planet? Grow up, Gutner.’

The boat is shrinking faster and faster as the aircraft rises up into the air.

‘You knew all along, didn’t you?’ she says.

She leans forward. As she does so, Tenebris realises that she has planned the whole operation from the start. She isn’t suffering from a bad back, she has been hiding her escape plan. On her back is a parachute. It has been hidden within the cushioned back of her seat, which she has cut out to accommodate it. The straps of the chute have been passed through slits cut into her jacket. The whole thing has been invisible.

‘You’ll need this,’ she says, tossing the grenade at his feet, ‘The pin is somewhere on the floor. And this.’ She rips the top of the cyclic off its shaft and throws it at him, then tumbles backwards out of the helicopter, pulling the ripcord of her parachute as she goes. The helicopter starts to spin.

How has he so misjudged her? She must have dismantled the joystick before he even reached the airport. The whole thing has been planned meticulously. He wants to shoot her. He wants to find the grenade. He wishes he could fly a helicopter. He knows that without the cyclic in place it is all too late.

The parachute opens immediately. Gutner steers away from the helicopter as quickly as she can. Her chances of surviving the impact of the explosion that is about to happen are small but, for Tenebris, the odds are much worse. She makes do with that, it’s better than nothing.

66

Calypso and Steve have heard the yacht pass over them. Calypso is sure that she spotted Sam at the back of the boat. Steve has other things on his mind.

The yacht engine stops. They hear it from a kilometre away.

'We have to go,' Calypso says.

'You go.'

Calypso eavesdrops Steve's echolocation clicks. He has spotted a squid. Food. So that's the reason. Not interested in having an argument, Calypso leaves him to it. As she rediscovers the sea of her infancy, the joys of being home are flooding through her. Every rock formation, every underwater cave and arch on the seafloor, every reef and cliff are precious to her, bringing back memories of a time long ago when she felt safe. She dives to the seabed, passing a drinks can half-buried in the sand. Human rubbish is in every sea. With a flick of her flukes she buries the can in sand and powers herself towards the low arch that she knows she will find beyond the reef. Through a forest of kelp then back up towards the surface.

She thinks of how her life has changed. The years of isolation, forced to perform as a slave to the will of others, are coming to an end. It isn't over yet, but at last she knows that it will end. Having watched Steve exploring the sea that he left when he was only three months old, she dares to hope that he too may be healed, that he may find a pod of other young males and learn to enjoy life. It will take time for them both to relearn the culture of their sea. In the course of the past few hours they have met only two members of the local pods, both young females Calypso has never met before, but she feels certain that others have survived the recent attacks by the mafia and that soon they will be welcomed by the wider group and that this group will include young males and older individuals who have known her parents.

The shadow of the yacht lies ahead of her on the sea floor.

A flash of light startles her. It is as if the sun has burst out from behind a cloud for an instant but the noise seconds later tells her this is not the sun but more man-made destruction. In her years wasted on combat missions she has witnessed plenty of explosions. Something crashes down onto the sea above her. All at once the surface is penetrated by dozens of falling lumps. Calypso turns tail and speeds away from the danger.

Something else falls into the waves. Large, red and soft, floating like a giant jellyfish. Flailing about, snared in the tentacles that trail beneath the jellyfish is a large creature that looks suspiciously human. Predator and prey are slowly sinking beneath the surface.

Calypso knows very well that this isn't a jellyfish, she has served in four wars and has seen more than one parachute smother a human landing on the sea before dragging him down to his death. In the hot shallow sea her orders were only to report the incident and never to get involved, but now she is not under orders, she is a free agent. Weaving a course between the pieces of debris sinking around her, Calypso swims to the human trapped in its parachute. The woman is engaged in a life or death struggle to free herself before she runs out of air. Without hesitation Calypso positions herself next to the woman, nudging her with her flipper and offering her dorsal fin. The woman turns. For a moment she is terrified then their eyes meet and she understands. She grabs Calypso's fin and, struggling desperately to supress the urge to breathe, allows herself be pulled towards the surface. It always amazes Calypso how short a period of time humans can survive underwater without artificial breathing apparatus. They are so vulnerable, or they are without their machines. With them, they are the most dangerous creatures in the sea.

She breaks the surface and nudges the woman out after her, hearing her snatch a huge lungful of air. The parachute is heavy with water. Calypso swims toward shallow water. She pokes her head up out of the water to catch the woman's eye.

'Hold on,' she says, speaking through her blowhole.

The woman looks afraid and Calypso isn't sure she has been understood. She powers towards a strip of beach, dragging the chute and the woman behind her. Seconds later, feeling the shingle rub her belly, Calypso wriggles free, leaving the woman on her hands and knees a couple of metres from dry land.

Behind her Vikki Gutner climbs to her feet, staring at the dorsal fin until it disappears from view. A thoughtful smile spreads across her face.

67

'It's her, I know it's her!' I jump up and down. 'Calypso!' I shout.

Sven and I are side by side at the stern of the boat staring at the shore. Of the helicopter only a few bits of plastic and a row of seating remain.

Tim emerges from under a table.

'I knew it,' he mutters, glowering at me and brushing imaginary dust from his jacket. 'I just knew it.'

The other crewman who welcomed us aboard appears, running.

'Mr Bronson has woken up, and he is not happy.'

'It's all over, boys,' Sven says breezily. 'You can relax.'

The second crewman makes to move my bag off the chair.

'Leave it,' I say 'I'll do it.'

We are saved an awkward moment by the arrival of Calypso who pops up in the water just a couple of metres from the yacht.

'Are you OK?' I sign.

She nods. In my bag are the hydrophone and tablet. I switch them both on and climb down the steps to the wooden platform just above the water.

'Who are these people?' Calypso asks.

I explain what has happened as best I can and tell her we have to go to France.

'How far is France?' Calypso asks.

'Tim?' I say.

Tim tries to pretend he hasn't been reading the tablet over my shoulder. I give him the look.

'Thirteen hours at ten knots,' Tim answers tersely. 'I heard the captain tell Mr Bronson.'

I pass the information on.

'I cannot swim at that speed for thirteen hours. We are already tired. I want to talk with Michel.'

Sven, who is also reading the tablet, dials Dad's number on his phone and passes it to me.

Dad answers.

'Dad it's me. Count to ten then talk really loudly for a few seconds.' I turn to Sven, 'how do you set it to full volume?'

Sven fixes the audio level and I lean forwards over the water, holding the phone to Calypso's ear. Dolphin ears are basically pretty small holes and I am not at all sure this will work. I hear the tiny squeak of Dad's shouting. Calypso moves in closer until her ear is touching the phone. For a moment it looks like the plan is an epic fail then Calypso emits a torrent of clicks and whistles so loud that I flinch backwards, almost dropping the phone in the sea. Eventually the noise subsides sufficiently for the software to translate.

'Michel, I have found my home. Every rock, every arch, every cave. My home sea. I want you to see and …'

'Hang on,' I sign. I put the phone to my ear. 'Dad, did you hear that?'

'I heard what sounded like a firework display in a cellar.'

'I'll translate.' I turn to Sven and the two crewmen. 'Can you give us a little space?'

Sven stretches out an arm. 'You can tell your father that Tenebris is dead,' he says, as he escorts the crewmen away.

'Who?'

'The man in the helicopter. Your Dad will understand. Persuade him to catch a flight to Nice.'

It isn't an easy conversation; phone down to sign to Calypso, read the tablet screen, pick up the phone, talk, listen, put down the phone, sign again …

Dad is shaken by the news of the car bomb. He explains that he and Sven persuaded an influential member of the Civil Liberties, Justice and Home Affairs Committee in the European Parliament to fly to Corsica along with two senior officials and an academic. They agreed to meet Calypso and Steve, with me to act as interpreter, to establish the validity of the claim that the two dolphins could communicate with humans and should therefore be considered sentient beings. It's only the beginning of a long process, but the deaths will put everything back coming, as they do, on top of the death of Carla Biseti, the MEP for Calabria, who was shot in the European Parliament building in Brussels the day she met Rafael and I.

'Why is Sven sure that Tenebris is dead?' Dad asks.

I explain the helicopter explosion a few minutes earlier.

'If he is right, that is a big relief. 3-TEC will need time to regroup so that is one less threat to worry about for the moment.'

'France is a very long swim,' Calypso says. 'Isn't there another way?'

'The car bomb might have nothing to do with your arrival, Corsican politics is complicated but, until they know for sure, no-one will come to meet you. Sven is right, you need to be away from the reach of the mafia. Destroying those tuna nets was not the smartest thing we did; it increased our list of enemies.'

'Michel, we had to save the pod.' Calypso says.

'I understand. Look, if Sven has got you on this boat, he must be able to persuade them to travel more slowly. I will see if I can get Lara transferred to Nice. Is Sven there?'

'He left.'

'Find him and get him to call me. In the meantime find Steve, he has to come with you.'

I cut the call and ask Calypso to find Steve. The yacht is huge. Eventually I bump into a chef carrying a cake in the shape of a fat lady in a banana costume. He takes me to Tim who escorts me to the bridge where Sven is talking with the ship's captain.

The captain has the relaxed face of a man who is always on holiday. Sitting in his huge blue leather armchair, facing a window that must be almost ten metres across above a battery of screens set into a hardwood table that stretches from one side of the yacht to the other, the captain strokes his beard patiently while Sven chats with Dad, and he keeps on stroking it while Sven explain what he wants.

'How about this?' the captain says. 'We sail at six knots for now then when Mr Bronson is up, which tends to happen around 2pm, I will suggest to him that the seas are a little choppy and that he will be more comfortable if we take things slowly. I anything changes I will make sure you are informed. Help yourselves to nuts and olives, by the way.'

'You don't think he'll mind?' I ask.

'Let you into a little secret, Dear. Our big problems on a ship like this sometimes stretch to concern about the lack of rocket in the lobster salad, or a little whinge about there not being an App to open the curtains in the state bedroom. Had a crisis last month because one member of crew was allegedly wearing noisy shoes. A few strips of felt and another major incident evaporated. As long as everything is paid for I can accommodate almost every whim. I have absolutely no idea why Mr Bronson decided to welcome you as his guests on our journey to Nice, it is none of my business. I will simply try to keep everyone happy for the duration, as long as you can reassure me that there aren't other helicopters queuing up to attack my ship.'

'About the décor in my bedroom …' I start.

'Cheeky,' says the captain.

68

With everything sorted, for a few hours at least, I go to my room to sleep. Then change my mind and go to Rafael's room. I grab a few cushions and lie on the floor by the huge bed, away from the door, my arms wrapped through the submersible bags so no-one can prise them away.

When Steve appeared with Calypso he dumped the two other bags onto the platform at the back of the yacht so we now have all our kit. We have been through too much to risk losing the laptops or any of the other equipment, maps and evidence that will be vital to proving our story if we ever meet anyone who is able to help us.

Remembering Fred and Keisha, I got up again and traipse across the corridor to their room, clutching my bags. The pair of them are sitting on the bed wrapped in blankets, Fred reading his Martian fantasy book and Keisha watching cartoons on the television.

'We're drying our things on the radiator,' Keisha announces. 'Did you know that one of the drawers is full of chocs,' she adds, making huge yummy eyes at me. 'I'll show you.' She jumps off the bed, still wrapped in her blanket, crosses to the dressing table and pulls open a drawer.

'They're the posh ones that are all runny in the middle but they're OK,' she says offering me a box.

I shake my head.

'Are you seasick?'

'I need to sleep.'

I can tell she doesn't see that as a valid reason for turning down free chocolate and, in normal circumstances ...

'Have you got Rafael's mobile in one of those bags?' she asks, changing tack. 'Only I was using it and that. And I thought I could charge it up for him. This room has lecky sockets and everything.'

If what Sven has said is true then we can all relax a little. I open the bags and find the phone and the charger.

'Boss,' she says, running back to the bed with it.

I poke Fred. He looks up.

'Are you OK?'

He shrugs. 'She keeps pestering me to watch TV.'

'I spoke with Dad. Mum's a little better.'

He glances briefly in my direction.

'And it sounds like Mr Bronson gets up at two so I imagine we will eat something then,' I sign and speak simultaneously.

'Is he famous?' Fred signs.

'He's rich. And I guess he's famous. He was the voice of the dog in that film we …'

'I want pasta.' Keisha says, taking my photo with Rafael's smart phone.

'I'm having a pizza, chips and apple pie.'

'And that pudding with the meringue and the cherries. Oh yeah.'

Ten minutes in a floating palace and the pair of them think they are royalty.

'Stay in your room and don't annoy anyone, OK? I'll see you later,' I say, pulling their door closed behind me.

Back in Rafael's room I curl up on the floor, clutching the bags, and fall asleep as soon as my head touches the cushion.

I awake to the sound of discrete tapping on the door. Rafael groans as he sits up, facing the door.

'Yes.'

The door opens.

'It's Rafael, isn't it?' Tim's voice plummy rings out. 'Mr Bronson has asked for everyone to join him for lunch at three in the green dining room. That's in fifty minutes. I've brought you some clothes. Tailored for the slimmer build.'

I sit up from behind the bed to see what he is talking about.

'Ah,' Tim says, adapting to the new situation. 'If you have a bad back, you will find the gym is well equipped and the masseur is available. Until ten o'clock. I'll leave the clothes here, shall I?'

'That's great,' Rafael replies. The rest and the antibiotics are doing their stuff and he is already looking a little better.

'Shall I bring Mademoiselle's options here?' Tim asks, depositing a pile of clothes on a table by one of the portholes.

'You can leave them in my room, thank you, Tim.' I answer then, in my poshest voice, 'That's absolutely marvellous.'

Tim pulls the door closed behind him.

'Absolutely marvellous?' Rafa says, mimicking my accent.

'You need the stethoscope to do it properly.'

We look at each other then burst out laughing and keep on laughing till the tears are rolling down our faces.

69

'So remind me exactly what you wish me to do, Mr…?'

'Sven will do, Wesley.'

We are sitting at a long table cut from a single green marble slab resting on an ornate golden frame. Besides us, there are Wesley Bronson, his secretary, Amelia Gorspan, and his publicist, Quinton Spell.

Wesley Bronson is at the head of the table, wearing a coral and turquoise dressing gown on top of his gold satin pyjamas. I realise I have seen him in several films. He seems smaller in real life than on the big screen, and is forever posing, presenting his face to an imaginary camera, blue eyes lingering on each of us in turn, like a butterfly flitting from flower to flower.

I decided against wearing one of the ball gowns that Tim the steward laid out across my bed and opted instead for wearing my jeans, though I have put on one of the white shirts left for Rafael. At my feet are the bags, I have counted at least six other people on board and I trust no-one.

While we pounce on the food, piling our plates high with chicken goujons, sauté potatoes, rice, salads, grilled fish, ratatouille, bread, cheese, vol au vents, you name it we eat it, Wesley Bronson only nibbles at a chicken leg then picks at a few olives and grapes.

Amelia Gorspan, who is thinner than a sheet of paper, seems to get all the calories she needs from watching us stuff ourselves. Quinton Spell, on the other hand, has a belly the size of a spacehopper and a hunger to match. I don't see him chew anything, he simply pushes food into his face, pausing only to gulp down huge mouthfuls of wine from a glass the size of a vase.

'As I said this morning, I am proposing the publicity event to end all publicity events,' Sven says. 'With you at its heart. Your philanthropy is well known, as is your generous and vocal support for GreenOcean which has done so much to alert the world to the multiple threats faced by the world's marine life …'

Listening to Sven is like listening to the judges on Strictly Come Dancing dribbling over a perfect foxtrot, an illusion reinforced by the fact that Sven is wearing a white tuxedo. It appears that he, like Rafael, has taken up the offer of dressing for lunch with items from the ship's wardrobe. If she saw him, my mum would say that Sven has completely disappeared up his own bottom, before quickly telling us that she has been very rude and that we must never repeat it in public.

'I know the media will be waiting for you when we dock in Nice and I was hoping you would say a few words about two amazing dolphins and their young friends here. I can guarantee you that it is a story that will be shown on every news channel around the world.'

'Mr Bronson is already on every news channel around the world,' Amelia Gorspan observes curtly.

'And deservedly so. This story will simply ensure that the world sees even more of him as he prepares to shoot Nice Work 2,' Sven counters.

Fifteen all.

'It might not be the kind of publicity that Mr Bronson needs at this time,' Gorspan insists.

Fifteen thirty.

For a moment Sven's face suggests he would quite like to open a window and toss Amelia Gorspan into the sea.

'How does my marine conservation endorsement play with twenty to forty four year olds in Europe, Quinton?' Wesley Bronson says, cutting in.

We wait while Quinton swallows a steak.

'The twenty to thirty quartile are huge fans, Sir. As you know, they are all over environmental messaging. Polar bears, whales, tropical rainforests, anything with fur, seaweed diets, free-range eggs, didgeridoos, you name it.' Quinton wipes mayonnaise from his mouth with a scarlet napkin and finishes a glass of wine. 'The thirty to forty four year old demographic broadly follow the same values, as long as you don't mention climate change. It doesn't play well with their SUV four-wheel drive owning, three-flying-holidays-a-year, buy-the-biggest-television lifestyles. But frankly, Sir, you go large on protecting dolphins and you are maintaining and developing positive profile across the board, from baby to grandma everywhere. Except in parts of Japan. It will play even better than buying that T-Rex skeleton in New York last year.'

'Doesn't sound too bad, Amelia?' Bronson turns to his secretary.

Amelia contents herself with staring up at the ceiling and sighing.

‘And you want these children on camera with me, and the dolphins? Are they all going to be jumping through hoops? Or are we against hoops and marine parks? Guys?’

‘With respect,’ Sven interjects. ‘This isn’t a story about marine parks. It is much bigger than that. These dolphins can talk.’

‘I don’t do quirky, do I, Quinton?’

‘Sam can talk with the dolphins and they talk back.’ Keisha says.

Bronson stares at Keisha as if he were noticing her for the first time.

‘Like a magic show?’ Bronson asks.

‘It’s not magic, it’s real,’ Keisha insists. ‘And it’s boss. They’re amazing and they saved our lives and everybody is trying to kill us because they don’t understand but one day everyone will chill out and dolphins and people will live together like they did in olden times.’

‘Is this true?’ Bronson turns to Fred who is taking photos of the cutlery with Rafael’s phone.

Keisha nudges Fred then, when she has his attention, points towards Bronson.

‘He’s not meff,’ Keisha explains to Bronson. ‘It’s just his lugs, they’re useless ‘cos he’s deaf. He’s all right with the lippies though, do you know what I mean?’

‘Is someone going to translate?’ Bronson asks.

Amelia Gorspan throws up her hands, she obviously hasn’t come across a Scouser before and hasn’t understood a word Keisha said.

‘Why don’t I introduce you to Calypso and Steve?’ I suggest, trying to get a grip on the situation.

‘What about you, Steve?’ Bronson says, looking at Rafael. ‘Are you the family accountant?’

Bronson has a point. Keisha, Fred and I have turned up for lunch in our own clothes, except for my use of a white shirt, but Rafael has reverted to type. Like Sven, Rafael has put on one of the suits Tim has brought to his room and he looks like he did when I first met him in the European Parliament nearly a month ago. Dark suit, caramel-coloured shirt with a beautifully knotted blue tie. He has even brushed his shaggy hair.

‘Steve and Calypso are the dolphins,’ Rafael explains. ‘And Keisha’s right, they do talk. We have this software Sam’s Dad developed with the dolphins. You have to use sign language but the dolphins talk back in clicks and whistles and the software …'

'Let me show you,' I say.

'I don't do scuba diving do I, Amelia? It's an insurance thing.'

'You don't have to get in the sea.'

'Then lead our first battle: worthy Macduff.' Bronson says, pushing back his chair, 'and we shall take upon us what else remains to do, according to our order.'

As we file out of the green dining room, Keisha grabs my sleeve.

'He needs a doctor, that one,' she observes seriously.

'Have you seen the doctor?' I ask.

Keisha shakes her head.

'Marvellous!' I say in my plummiest voice.

70

'So tell me, Mr Sven, what is the angle for tomorrow?' Wesley Bronson asks as he stands back from the dolphins, finds and chair and sits down.

'How about Film star, Wesley Bronson, saves unhappy dolphins from life of abuse,' suggests Amelia Gorspan.

'Not good, not good,' says Quinton, who is chewing on a couple of chicken legs he took from the green dining room and now clutches in his right fist. 'The A word does not play well with the entertainment demographic. Nice Work as Bronson saves desperate dolphins. How does that sound?'

Bronson turns to me. 'What do you think, kid?'

I look over at Sven. It is a nightmare. The more I see, the more I realise that Wesley Bronson is interested in only one thing: himself.

The captain has stopped the yacht. Bathed in weak sunlight on the platform at the stern, I have introduced Bronson to Calypso and Steve, explaining to them that he is a famous person who will enable us to speak with the world's media. Calypso asks if he knows how many tuna are being killed in the Mediterranean. Quinton pushes in, using his vast belly like an icebreaker, suggesting that the killing angle won't go down well with the television channels and that maybe we need something brighter and more family orientated.

'And let's change the name Steve to …' Quinton starts.

'Wesley,' Bronson suggests then seems to consider the possibility that he might have gone too far. 'Flukey?'

'No, Wesley is good,' Quinton says, obsequiously. 'Wesley meets Wesley. I like it. Hell, you have a top grossing movie right there.'

I glare at Sven. He has to step in and stop this nonsense before I scream. Next to Sven, Keisha is taking photos on Rafael's smart phone. How many pictures has she taken? Does she even know how to use the camera?

'I'm thinking maybe just the two younger children next to you,' Quinton continues. 'Sam here is a bit tall for a girl, and the multicultural and learning difficulties angles play well to your compassion.'

'It's the flower festival in Nice, Sir,' Amelia Gorspan cuts it. She has stayed back, well away from the dolphins, clearly uncomfortable and muttering about catching diseases. 'Maybe if they could be trained to present you with bunches of flowers?'

Bronson claps his hands. 'Oh … oh … yes … That is perfect!' He gets off his chair and pats Calypso on the beak then steps back. 'We are going to have such fun everyone!' He climbs off the platform and back up onto the deck. 'Can you ask Maurice to look at colours? I am not sure what goes best with dolphin grey. A eggplant purple suit, perhaps?'

'What do they call that colour? Aubergine? Is that it?' Bronson is saying as he walks away with Gorspan beside him, taking notes.

'Do they eat chicken bones?' Quinton asks, gazing down at the dolphins.

'What?' I say sharply.

'Don't get eggy with him, Sam,' Keisha advises. 'He could start a fight in an empty house, that one.'

Having failed to get an answer, Quinton drops the bones on the table and waddles off.

We all stand there staring at each other, lost for words.

'Total weirdness scenario,' Rafael speaks for the first time in twenty minutes.

'Are you sure this is going to work?' I say to nobody in particular.

I haven't translated most of what Bronson and his aides have said but the emotional sense of dolphins is more highly developed than that of humans and Calypso has read our body language like a book.

'Are they bad people,' Calypso asks, 'or octopuses?'

Have I just heard my first dolphin metaphor? 'If octopus means mad then yes to that,' I sign.

'The skinny woman is bad,' Fred signs.

'It is a waste of time,' Steve says. 'Let's go.'

'Calm down, everyone,' Sven steps in. 'I have never pretended to anybody that this would be easy. Everyone is only interested in themselves. No-one wakes up thinking I wonder if anything interesting is happening between humans and dolphins. You have to … we have to make friends with people who have power. We have to be clever. It would be just the same if you were talking with politicians, or scientists, or religious leaders, or even the people who run GreenOcean. They all have egos, they all have their own agendas.

If you want to change the world you have to stand and fight, and you need a plan.'

While Keisha and Fred play on deck, the five of us, Sven, Rafael, Calypso, Steve and I spend ten minutes planning how to make best use of any media opportunity that takes place when we dock in Nice, before being interrupted by Tim who tells us curtly that the captain is powering up the engines.

The sun is dipping into the sea and darkness is sweeping in from the east as we gather our things and head inside.

71

The rest of the afternoon is almost boring though, given the events of the past forty eight hours, we are all fairly comfortable with boring. Fred reads his book, and Keisha watches films in their pink and gold palace. Rafael and I sit on his bed watching the news on the giant television in his room.

The car bomb attack outside Bastia is receiving coverage on the French news channels but the international news stations barely mention it.

The French news report picks up that the bombing represents the second killing of a member of the European Parliament in a month. They also note that mafia gangs may be implicated in both killings. Given that MEP Carla Biseti's death in Brussels came in the wake of her work to tackle illegal tuna fishing activities in the Mediterranean, could the death in Corsica be linked to the same thing? The representative of the Corsican police believes the deaths are more likely to be part of the Fronte di Liberazione Naziunale Corsu's long running campaign for an independent Corsica.

The next news item is a story about how a man bought a secondhand recipe book and found tucked between the pages a dozen letters that a woman had written to her son but never sent. The man has contacted the son and taken the letters to him. It gets me thinking.

'Rafael, why don't you ring your mum?' I say. 'It must be safe from here on the ship. She must be worried. Have you even spoken to her since your Dad … I know you said she is always too busy but …'

'I lied to you, Sam.'

'What do you mean?'

Rafael lowers his eyes.

How often has he spoken with her since we took la Vita Nuova and started our journey northwards? Why has he kept it a secret? He is the one who keeps saying we are all in this together and there he is making calls on his mobile that could potentially be traced and put us all in danger. Without telling us?

Rafael is fiddling with one of the tassels on a cushion, twisting it in his fingers. He gives me a brief sidelong glance and sighs. I wait.

'She's dead, Sam. She died three years ago.'

'But you said …'

'I know. I didn't wait to talk about it so I just told you she was never there.' He gathers his thoughts. Twice his lips part as if he is about to speak but no sound comes out. 'She was beautiful. I loved her with all my heart. I still do.' He swallows. 'When Dad wasn't bullying me, he was bullying her. She hid it well, but I saw it happening. He would shout at her and beat her. Over nothing at all. He was always clever about it. Never her face, never somewhere that people would see. Not at the start.'

Rafael lies back on the bed, staring at the ceiling. 'When Dad came home really happy, those was the worst times. He would arrive with a big box of cakes and a bunch of flowers for Mum, and sometimes a present for me. He'd be laughing and saying we should eat out on the terrace, to celebrate, and Mum would move everything outside and we would sit down while he talked about how Italian football was the best in the world or something like that. Little by little, the mood would change and it would become clear that he had not had a great day but a terrible day and all the presents and laughter were a front, an attempt to sound cheerful. And all it took was one tiny mistake from Mum or me, not smiling properly at one of his jokes or not being excited enough about the flowers or the presents, and he would flip and become a monster.'

I climb off the bed and switch off the television. 'Why didn't you tell us?'

'One day, after Christmas three years ago, he hit her in the face. Over nothing at all. She had sighed too loudly he said. Mum stood up and left the room.'

I am standing by the bed. Rafael sits up and stares at the wall.

'I didn't even hear the front door open. Hours later, I was in bed when the police arrived. She had been hit by a car on a roundabout.' He thinks for a moment. 'I was happy when he was thrown out of that helicopter.'

'No, you weren't,' I say. 'Because you're not like your Dad. Nothing like him. What was your Mum's name?'

'Alessandra,' he whispers, wiping his eyes.

There is a knock on the door. It is Tim, to tell us we will be eating in the blue dining room. Mr Bronson is tired and will be eating in his rooms. Tim hands out menus and invites us to choose what we want. If he notices Rafael's red eyes he keeps it to himself. After Tim has gone I squeeze Rafa's hand and ask him if he is OK and he says he is and I go back to my room to sort myself out before we go to eat.

Sven eats with us but seems as tired as we are. Only Fred and Keisha are really hungry, grabbing at everything on the table so greedily that I keep my hands out of sight. To be on the safe side.

Sven reminds Rafael and I that we have to think very carefully about what we want to say to the world's media in the morning.

'You only get one shot at this, kids, so make sure it's good,' he says. 'Did you check out the stuff on those memory sticks I gave you?'

We shake our heads. Sven gives me the kind of look and wry smile that Mum gives me when I explain that I don't need to do my homework because someone has said that the teacher won't be in tomorrow.

'What should we say?'

'That's not my job, Sam. It's yours. The only advice I have for you both is to speak from the heart. Tell them what you really feel. The world is full of phonies, people who only say what they think others want to hear, people who will say anything in order to get their own way, people who speak without considering the meaning of the words they use. That's why the world is as it is.'

Sven pushes his chair back and puts his feet up on the table.

'Take Mr Wesley Bronson here, he has no opinions about anything. I was a fool; I misread him completely. I saw stuff on the internet about him supporting GreenOcean and their campaign to save the seas and I decided that Wesley Bronson cared about the planet. But the guy is only greenwashing his media image, building a profile to manipulate young people into going to his movies. And he is not alone.'

'Even the super-rich don't do what they want to most of the time. They just do the things super-rich people are meant to enjoy doing. Does anyone really like this kind of furniture and these fat carpets and these crystal glasses? Why do they buy diamond encrusted freezer bags and platinum pillowcases? They are all playing the game, trying to look right in front of other people. It's expensive, it must be good. It's rare, it must be special. If I have it then I must be good and special. Am I making sense?'

'Sort of.' I say.

'Yes,' Rafael says purposefully.

'And before you feel smug, we are all the same. You don't know why you like this toothpaste more than that toothpaste, any more than Mr Bronson does. But you do know why those dolphins are special and why they matter to the rest of the world. Now you just have to convince everyone else.'

Sven takes his feet off the table and stands up.

'Good luck to both of you.' And with that he leaves the room.

'Sounds like you two need thinking doughnuts,' Keisha says thoughtfully. 'They probably have them on this boat. Gold plated ones with tiny china handles. Shall we call Tetchy Tim?'

I smile and shake my head. 'It's going to take more than thinking doughnuts to sort this out.'

'How about a massive thinking cake? The size of a car? Like you could sit in it and …' Her voice tails off. She turns to Fred and pokes him. 'Do yer want to take some of this chicken back to our room and watch cartoons of the gogglebox?'

Fred nods yes about the food but pulls his book out of his pocket; he would rather read than watch television.

Keisha kisses her teeth in frustration.

They pile a plate with cakes and deep fried chicken and, shortly before ten o'clock, we all leave the dining room and go to our rooms. Rafael and I agree we will meet at seven thirty to show each other what we have written, and that is that.

For a while I sit at my table scribbling. I draw a word cloud like we are taught in English at school, writing words like dolphins … language … our world … precious … intelligent … sea … resources … fish … common future …

I write Ladies and Gentlemen I would like to start by … several times.

I write The world is under threat and unless …

It is all rubbish. What can you say to convince a bunch of people who don't care about anything other than their own lives and immediate needs to wake up and think about the miracle of being alive on a world that contains all the amazing beauty that this one contains? How do you get people who have never spoken to their next-door neighbours to think about the needs of another species? How do you persuade people who are struggling to look after their families to think of those who will live after they are dead? How do you convince religions and governments and businesses to consider the rights of beings who live in the sea? It is hopeless. I am only sixteen and I have tears rolling down my face as I think of how unequal I am to the task. After an hour I give up and go to bed, telling myself that I will get up at six and write my speech when my thoughts are clear.

I switch the lights off but cannot sleep. The table I pushed in front of the door, so that no-one can get in, isn't helping. Maybe it is the heat, maybe it is because I know that in the morning I am going to make an idiot of myself. Whatever. I get up and open both portholes to let some air circulate then lie back down on the bed.

A thin cool current of air brushes my cheek. I find myself thinking of the night I spent in the mountain cabin on the Italian border about three weeks ago, surrounded by thick snow. I was similarly worn out then, having escaped my pursuers on their snowmobiles by jumping on a stag's back for a terrifying rush through a pine forest. How many deer had there been in that herd? Twenty, thirty, forty … I try to remember …

In a fraction of a second I am fully alert. My watch tells me it is three fifty six. I have slept for several hours. The smell of wood polish hangs in the air and I remember where I am. What has woken me? The gentle vibration of the ship's engines is still there. Is it a little louder than before?

Relax girl, everything is OK.

The faint light from the portholes reflects off the polished wood surfaces of the cabin, giving the whole room a ghostly monochrome glow. It is like being on a film set.

My bags!

I reach out a leg, the bags are still there. Placing my head back on the pillow, I close my eyes and I am beginning to drift when I hear a loud burst of whistles and clicks. Up in a flash, I race to the nearest porthole and peer out. The sea is still calm.

'Calypso, is that you?'

More whistles and clicks. Something is wrong.

72

Unable to see the water close to the yacht, I know I have to go outside. I haul the table away from the door. Bags in hand and barefoot, I tiptoe down the corridor and out on deck. A light comes on automatically, if there are also alarms I am in trouble. I hurry aft, hoping the lights will switch themselves off after a minute or so, when the sensors stop detecting movement.

There is something different, but what? I sit down at one of the tables and wait, quite still. After maybe thirty seconds the light changes, but not down on the lower deck where I am. A light has gone off higher up. Which means that someone else has been moving about. Turning my wrist I check the time. Three forty am.

Three minutes later the lights outside the door I used to come out on deck are still on. Looking south the view is awesome. In a cloudless sky, the Milky Way stretches from one horizon to the other, millions of stars in a view so huge it is scary.

A liquid sound to my left causes me to turn around. I quickly pull the hydrophone out of a bag and lower it into the water while I rummage for the tablet.

'You have to slow the boat. Calypso is tired and cannot keep up,' the screen reads when it has booted up. 'Why are you going faster?'

That's it. The engine hum has changed. But the captain promised to tell us if the yacht changed speed.

Get real, Sam, like he has to tell you what he is doing.

'Sam, Sam.'

'Yes, Steve, I heard you. I'll go and investigate.'

'Hurry.'

'I'll be back as soon as I can,' I reassure him, pulling the hydrophone out of the water and stuffing everything back in the bag. As I make my way back along the deck the lights switch off. I check my watch. Three forty two.

I approach the door with my back to the outside wall of the cabins but the light comes on just the same. If they all stay on for five minutes after they have been triggered then it means that whoever triggered the light on the deck above passed the sensor only minutes before I woke up. Back in the gloom of the corridor, lit only by a solitary night light at floor level at the far end, I gently open Rafael's door. It opens about two centimetres then stops.

'Rafael,' I hiss through the gap. 'Rafael.'

'What?' he answers groggily.

'You need to get up.'

Secondly later I hear the sound of something heavy being dragged away a few centimetres at a time. The door opens.

'Are you scared of the dark or something?' I say. 'We have to go to the bridge.'

'You've been listening to too many old James Brown songs.'

'Who?'

'I feel good, nana nana nana na.' Rafael sings. 'Let's go to the bridge, nana nana nana na.'

'What? Listen to me. Someone has changed the speed. The dolphins can't keep up. We have to find the pilot's room, the captain's …'

'It's OK, the bridge was fine, I understand. I'll find my shoes.'

'No, barefoot is better.'

Rafael steps out into the corridor. He is still wearing his shirt and tie.

He takes one of the bags and we hurry away from the cabins, past the dining room and up the stairs to the top deck. In the semi-darkness we find the door to the bridge. It is slightly ajar. Cautiously, we push it open and slip inside.

It doesn't require a Sherlock Holmes to work out which computer terminal has been tampered with. Of the five display screens, three are in sleep mode.

The fourth shows a map of blue sea and the south coast of France, and the fifth displays a virtual instrument panel and, in a white box covering a quarter of the screen, the words 'manual override initiated' in large flashing red letters.

'Whatever you do, don't trigger an alarm. We do not want to be caught.'

'Really?' Rafael replies, his head bowed over the controls and levers in front of the display.

'I suppose you are now going to tell me you have piloted a luxury yacht.'

'The controls are basically the same as the ones on La Vita Nuova,' he explains, without looking up. 'Just more sophisticated. You can do it, if you want. These small levers are digital versions of …'

'No, no, you do it.'

Rafael touches the display screen, clicking on various boxes until he finds what he is looking for. He pulls back on the levers set into the desk.

'That's it. I've set it back to five knots. It was up at twelve. Didn't the captain say …'

'He set it at six knots. Sven and I watched him do it and he told us that if anything changed he would inform us.'

'Did he know about the dolphins?'

'We didn't explain in detail, but he must know.'

'Weird.'

'The lights were on outside on the top deck when I came out. Someone else has been moving about. Can you lock the speed setting so that it can't be changed.'

'I could try but we might wake the entire ship if I trip an alarm.'

'Forget it.'

The change in the ship's engine note is obvious as we step out into the corridor, slower and more rhythmic. We are halfway down the stairs when Rafael spots a shadow moving ahead of us. As quietly as we can, we race back upstairs and press ourselves into the darkness of an alcove opposite the door to the bridge. Moments later a figure appears at the top of the stairs.

73

Rafael steps out of the shadows and, before the figure standing at the door of the bridge is able to turn, strikes a glancing blow on the back of their head with the butt of the handgun which he has taken from the bag. The figure crumples to the floor.

'That's the second time you've done that. You'll end up murdering someone,' I say.

He feels for a pulse. 'Grab the legs.'

We enter the bridge a second time, closing the door behind us. A roll of packing tape later, we regain control of the situation.

'Where are we going to put her?'

'We need to find a cupboard,' Rafael answers. 'Somewhere that no-one will enter until after we have left the boat.'

'I know somewhere but it's right down the other end.'

'She's so skinny we won't even know we are carrying her.'

I am not so sure, but soon we are down on the aft deck, and Rafael is pulling on his inhaler.

'It's one of these.' I try the doors. The second door opens.

We carry Amelia Gorspan into the storeroom and lay her on the floor then stack scuba tanks and jackets in front of her. We have taped her ankles together with the packing tape, bound her wrists together behind her back, and taped her mouth, taking care to ensure her nose is clear. The noise of the engines is louder at the back of the boat so even if she wakes up before we leave the boat her moans will be hard to hear. It is ten past four.

'Why did she do it?' Rafael asks.

'She must have decided that we are nothing but trouble. If the dolphins aren't there in the morning then we have no story. Or maybe it's between Quinton and her. He thinks it's a good idea, she doesn't. I don't know.'

Our discussion is interrupted by a blast of clicks and whistles. We hurry aft and are both relieved to find Calypso and Steve have caught up and are now swimming behind the boat.

74

The adrenalin is pumping. I give up trying to sleep. Instead I lie on the bed with the television on, sound muted, going over and over what has happened in the past month, thinking about when we first met the dolphins and how we have slowly got to know each other.

The longer I lie there, on my poached egg patterned bed cover, the more I realise that I now think of both Calypso and Steve as people.

What does that mean? Can you be a person while not being a human being? What is a person? Does a person have to be able to walk? What does that make disabled humans? Does a person have to be able to speak? What does that make Fred? Does a person have to have a sense of history and culture? Do dolphins have those things?

When Calypso explained about visiting the cave and being taken there by older members of the pod she was talking about culture, something the dolphins teach each other, an experience they pass on from generation to generation. Travelling to the cave through the tunnels teaches the young dolphins how to use echolocation, but they can learn how to use echolocation anywhere and the cave itself serves no practical purpose, it is a cultural experience, an opportunity to hear the strange acoustics of the space. Is that right?

And when the dolphin caught in the pen called Calypso by her mother's name it brought memories and emotions flooding back to Calypso, just as it Rafael's mother's name does to him.

The obvious difference between us and the dolphins is not our ability to reason or our capacity to form emotional bonds with others but our bodies and our relationship with possessions. Dolphins travel light; apart from the sponges certain dolphins use to protect their snouts when foraging on the seafloor, or the conch shells they use to help them fish, and other similar stuff Dad had told me about, they use few things. Human lives, on the other hand, are wrapped up in things. Without things we cannot even step outside because we are naked. Without cars, buses, or trains many humans cannot travel to work or to school or to the shop to buy food. Our houses are full of things that we use to tell ourselves and other humans who we are. My mobile, my television, my DVD, my computer, my sofa, my kitchen, my hat … the list is absolutely endless. We are our things. To not have many things is to be poor. To be poor is bad.

I remember learning about rainforest pygmies in human geography, how they have few possessions and build temporary homes out of sticks and leaves, and how we all felt sorry for them and called them primitive.

There is a knock on the door. Six o'clock. It is Rafael; he can't sleep either. I drag the table away and invite him in. He arches an eyebrow but offers no comment on the table behind the door thing, which is sweet. We talk and talk.

We remember the memory sticks Sven mentioned. We shove one into a USB port on one of the laptops. Many of the files are stuff we are already aware of. The laptop we are using is one of Dad's, it's packed with files about the dolphin programme and secret stuff about navy missions in the Arabian Gulf.

The memory stick also contains various videos, including the ones Z showed us on the train when we were fleeing Brussels three weeks ago. There is the film showing the dying man lying on a beach, with the sea dragon tattooed on his calf and ankle. The same tattoo Dad has on his leg, as the property of the 3-TEC marine counter-surveillance programme. There is a film showing a large pool set in a dry rocky landscape with brilliant sunshine creating harsh black shadows.

The last film we click and open shows a wide-angle view of room with a table laid out with sandwiches and drinks. Long curtains are hanging along one wall. We hid behind those curtains I realise with a shock. A door opens and two stocky men step into the room, followed by an elegantly dressed woman. Carla Biseti. The Member of the European Parliament. We watch in silence as the scene unfolds. The argument, the gun. We see the curtains billow gently as we make our escape through the door behind the curtains and one of the men races across the room and reveals the door and fiddles with the handle that Rafael is clinging on to on the other side of the door. We realise how close we were to witnessing Biseti's murder, which occurs seconds later on the film.

'This must be from a CCTV camera in the parliament. How did Sven get hold of it?' Rafael says.

‘We can’t just hand it over to the media. It should go to the police.’

Rafael shrugs.

At seven when the first pre-dawn light is permeating the eastern sky we go outside and find Steve and Calypso and I talk with them about the sea while they follow the yacht. Rafael sits quietly, lost in thought.

By a quarter to eight the sun is rising and we look round to the north and see the French coast up ahead. Tim appears, to tell us breakfast is in the blue dining room and to ask if we want coffee, tea or hot chocolate. We pack our equipment and leave the dolphins. As we pass the storeroom we hear a crash followed by a groan. I check that the storeroom door is closed, we just have to hope no-one else comes down that end of the boat before we dock.

75

Sven hears Rafael and Sam pass his room and waits. Satisfied the coast is clear, he conducts a final check of the bedroom and the bathroom to ensure he isn’t leaving anything behind, then slips out into the corridor, carrying his shoes.

He reaches the lower deck without being seen, pulls open the store room door and slips inside. Scanning the room he quickly finds what he is looking for, using the narrow beam from the LED torch on his key ring. The yacht reaches port in roughly an hour. If he commits himself now there will be no turning back, no plan B. On the other hand, within forty minutes the yacht will be close enough to land to take immediate action, if he is ready. That settles it; he will wait.

Having set his watch, Sven sits on the floor, adopts a yoga position and focuses on slowing his breathing. He is in a state of almost total relaxation when he hears a muffled groan very close by and to his right.

76

Having eaten breakfast, we are back on deck watching the approach to the harbour at Nice. Keisha is jumping up and down, having spotted a row of carnival floats parked up on the edge of the harbour. A four metre high blue elephant, a giant Volkswagen camper van, a collection of fairy tale characters, and a massive astronaut are glowing in the morning sunshine, in readiness for the afternoon's festivities.

'Where's Fred?' I ask Keisha.

'Being boring. Just sitting there on the bed, reading his book.'

'Go and fetch him. He needs to see this.'

Keisha sighs dramatically and runs off.

We have seen several dolphins and I panic, worrying that I will turn to introduce the dolphins only to find they aren't Calypso and Steve but two wild dolphins that I can't communicate with at all then, a kilometre from shore, two dolphins race up to the yacht and click their names and I relax.

Rafael is back in jeans and a t-shirt. He has found a cool pair of sunglasses to hide behind and is looking more relaxed than he must be feeling.

I am still clutching two of the submersible bags; Rafael has the other. I go over and over in my head what I will say once Wesley Bronson has said his piece. I ask Steve and Calypso to stay close by while I am speaking so that they can talk with the media.

We haven't seen Mr Bronson since lunch, almost sixteen hours ago. Is he still going to introduce us?

'He won't come. He says he wants to finish the chapter.' Keisha announces, racing up to me, out of breath.

Quinton Spell appears on deck looking for Tim and Amelia Gorspan. He is agitated and preoccupied.

'You kids ready for this? Journalists and camera crews have the attention span of sardines. While they can see the bait on the end of your line they're with you. Leave them for twenty seconds without input and they're gone, man. They're gone.'

‘They catch sardines in nets, Quinton,’ I say. ‘Have you ever been fishing?’

‘Nets, schmets. The point is that …’

‘Will you excuse me?’ I wave and hurry away to find Fred before Quinton can bore me to death.

The yacht slows right down as we draw near the jaws of the harbour. Waves slapping back from the harbour walls cause us to roll about a bit and I stagger down the steps and along the corridor to the bedrooms.

Fred is sprawled across the bed, his nose buried in the sands of Mars and the collapse of the thingian empire. I poke him.

‘There are amazing floats up on the harbour wall. We’re about to dock.’

He puts the book down briefly to sign. ‘Just finishing this chapter.’

‘We have to get ready to meet the media.’

‘I’m reading.’ He picks the book back up.

I tap him on the shoulder. ‘Come on, Fred. Forget fantasy worlds. There’s two dolphins to save. There’s a real world to protect. ‘ I take the book from him.

I hear the booming horn of a large cruise ship. Our yacht answers. Through the window I see sailors by bollards on the quayside, busy loosening the lines that hold the cruise ship in place. We pass into the harbour and the movement of the yacht changes, we are no longer at sea.

‘No-one needs me. I can’t talk to anyone,’ Fred signs. ‘I’m not important.’

‘Don’t be a prima donna. Keisha needs you. We all need you.’

Fred sighs dramatically and climbs off the bed. I steer him out of the bedroom, up the stairs and out on deck. Keisha spots us, races up to Fred and drags him away to look at something.

Tall apartment blocks rise up to our right and, by the harbour wall to our left, a huge red crane towers above us. The harbour is the largest we have visited since leaving the island of Lipari weeks ago.

How many reporters will there be? Do they really come out in their hundreds every time a film star turns up? What if no-one is there?

The yacht turns a corner to reveal another half a kilometre of harbour stretching ahead. In the distance are dozens of small boats, pleasure boats, rowing boats. On either side are a handful of larger yachts like our own and, finally, gathered on the quay maybe forty metres ahead are a group of reporters, photographers and three camera crews.

How many are there because the star of Nice Work is arriving to shoot a sequel and open the carnival, and how many are there because of the dolphins? Has Sven left it to Quinton to make the calls or has he made some himself? Come to think of it where is Sven?

There are people everywhere. Imagining the scene in the middle of the night, I was sure that the presence of crowds of people would guarantee our safety. Now I am not so sure. Any one of the hundred or more people waiting on the quayside could be a killer or an assassin. I think of the mafia thugs, the fishermen, the woman in the helicopter. Could I pick any them out in a crowd? Are the reporters really reporters? My fingers grip the gunwale so hard my knuckles turn white.

I feel a hand on my shoulder.

'It's OK, Sam,' Rafael says. 'We're doing this together.' He has pushed his sunglasses up and is smiling sweetly. I realise that he doesn't always look nerdy. In fact …

'All for one and one for all,' Keisha pokes her head round from behind Rafael's back. Fred emerges beside her. He has cheered up.

'We are Pod,' Fred signs, reaching out his hand.

'We're the Pod,' I agree. 'Or we will be when Calypso and Steve join us.'

'Look.' Keisha points down at the water.

Two dorsal fins have just broken the surface of the water.

Fred pulls his hand away from mine. 'What's that boat doing?'

On the other side of the yacht, a boat the size of La Vita Nuova is pulling up alongside us. As the back of the boat comes into view we read the words Gendarmerie Maritime in big letters along the hull. Two police officers are standing on deck and looking towards Quinton who has appeared out of nowhere. Quinton is gesticulating. Although he is facing away from us, we see his finger pointing us out to the police. The police look towards us and nod at Quinton.

77

At the same moment another person arrives on deck. Wesley Bronson is in a purple suit. He seems simply totally unaware of the police boat. Seeing us, he strides forwards all smiles, arms open wide, in full view of the cameramen and film crews standing on the quayside, less than fifteen metres away. Keisha glances at me, grabs Fred, and together they run to Wesley, allowing themselves to be scooped up in his arms. Cameras flash, reporters call out from the quayside.

'Mr Bronson, over here.'

'Are you happy to be back in Nice, Mr Bronson?'

'Looks like Nice Work, Mr Bronson!'

'Monsieur Bronson, par ici. Un sourire avec les enfants.'

'Are the children in the movie, Wesley?'

On the other side of the yacht, the police are looking uncomfortable, as is Quinton who has thrown his hands in the air and appears uncertain what to do next.

Rafael takes my hand. 'Forget the police.'

He drags me forwards until we are standing beside Wesley Bronson.

'Wave at the crowd,' Rafael says out of the corner of his mouth. 'Come on, Sam.' He smiles broadly for the cameras and waves, then leans forwards. 'Thanks, Mr Bronson, you don't know how much this means to us.'

'That's OK, Steve. I am happy to help. You young people are some of my biggest fans.' Seeing me, Bronson beams his most photogenic smile. 'Do you think you could try to be just a little bit shorter,' he says, gesturing a downward movement with his hand. 'Don't want you looking like a freak, do we?

Rafael glares at me. I bite my tongue, flex my knees and drop down a little. It isn't me who is the freak, it's Bronson, our Hollywood star who is anxious about being discovered to be shorter than his publicity material claims. Come to think of it, he is four or five centimetres taller than he was when we first met. I guess he must be wearing hidden heels.

‘OK, happy family! When I give the call we all shout Nice Work, right? Three, two , one …’

‘Nice Work.’ We all shout.

‘And again, three, two, one …’

‘Nice Work!’

Keisha is in her element, leaping up into the air as she shouts. Fred mimes, but the cameras won’t know that.

Behind us, the police appear to be losing interest. Quinton is protesting. I assume that he or Amelia had a change of heart about the whole dolphin story and tipped off the police with a story of stowaways or something.

The yacht’s berthing manoeuvre is almost complete and we are only a couple of metres from the quay.

‘What about the dolphins, Sir? How do you want to introduce them?’ Rafael asks.

I can’t get over how Rafael is taking charge of everything. He is awesome.

‘Let’s not push that for now, son,’ Bronson replies, still smiling for the cameras.

Tim and the other crewman whose name I never bothered to ask are opening a gate in the gunwale. A couple of other crewmen throw ropes towards harbour workers on the quayside.

‘But you promised that …’

‘Let me do my thing, Steve. Then, when they have all got their pictures, we’ll see …’

Bronson is using us for his media show then dumping us and we are powerless to stop him.

‘What about the dolphins, Mr Bronson?’ shouts a female voice in the pack of reporters..

Bronson looks taken off-guard. Cameras flash.

‘We hear that these children are travelling with dolphins that have learned to talk with humans?’ says another voice out of sight in the crowd. ‘Have you spoken with them yet?’

Good old Sven must have contacted the press and briefed them himself. How has he done it? Where is he?

‘As an active supporter of GreenOcean, you must be thrilled at being able to offer your support,’ says a news presenter standing next to a video camera crew. ‘How important a moment do you think this is for humanity?’

'Les dauphins, Monsieur Bronson. Ils sont où? Where are they?'

A gangplank is pushed out from the quayside and lands on the yacht's deck.

Bronson glances at me. He looks furious; rolled over by a bunch of kids. Now he has no option but to play the game. He turns back to the cameras, smile blazing, and strides along the gangplank off the yacht and into the media throng. We troop after him.

Bronson stops in front of the news crews. The sticker on one camera reads TF1, French news. The second is from euronews, and the third has 2DF or ZDF written on it and a German flag.

'It is great to be back in Nice,' Bronson starts. 'I am afraid the story of the dolphins may have been a little exaggerated.

That is it. I snap, step forward next to Bronson and speak directly to the cameras.

'No, it hasn't been exaggerated. The dolphins are here and you can all see for yourselves that human beings are, for the first time in our history, finally able to converse with another species. Follow me and I'll show you.'

I push my way through the crowd until I am level with the back of the yacht, unzip one of the bags and produce the hydrophone and the tablet. The news crews have followed me and the red lights are glowing on the front of the cameras. They are still filming.

'My Dad has worked with two dolphins for nine years and together they have learned to communicate using a mixture of sign language and a software that translates dolphin clicks and whistles into English. The dolphins have had to adjust their vocalisations (had I got that right?) so that they are in our human hearing range.'

I lower the hydrophone on its lead into the water, wrap the cable round a bollard to secure it, then switch on the wireless routing.

'Where are the dolphins?' someone calls out.

'They are in the water by the boat,' I reply.

Where are you? Calypso, Steve, please, please surface now.

Rafael, Keisha, and Fred join me, all looking down into the water. Nothing. I can feel the mood beginning to change. I have no choice. I pass Rafael the tablet.

'Pray that this works,' I say quietly, then jump off the quayside into the water.

The water is a little dirty but visibility is OK. To my left is the back end of the yacht. Behind me is the wall of the quay. A few fish are meandering about, but that is it. No sign of either Calypso or Steve. They have vanished. Has something frightened them off? Still underwater I swim round in a circle. Nothing. All that effort only to fall at the last hurdle.

I give up trying to stay underwater and allow my body to rise to the surface. Forty people stare down at me treading water.

'I'm sorry,' I splutter. 'I don't know what has happened. I promise you that they were …'

Suddenly the water bursts open on either side of me.

I know their smiles aren't smiles, just the shape of the beaks, but my smile is for real. I hug them both then swam to the platform at the back of the yacht and climb out of the water.

'Where have you been?' I sign and speak simultaneously so that dolphins and humans can all understand.

Calypso answers with a stream of whistles and clicks.

The camera crews are filming everything.

Rafael, who is holding the iPad, reads aloud from the screen, 'We were waiting for you to tell us it was safe.'

There is an outbreak of applause above us.

'This is your chance, this is our chance, to show the world that we are one,' I sign and speak.

Rafael, reads Calypso's response from the screen. 'I hope so, Sam, but I don't know whether humans are ready to share the world with us.'

One of the camera crews is filming the computer screen.

A burst of whistles and clicks from Steve. Rafael reads aloud from the screen. 'We want to live with you but you empty the sea of fish, you catch us and kill us, you train us to kill for you.'

'This is rubbish,' shouts a voice in the crowd. 'It's not real, just a phoney magic trick.' A fat man barges to the front, pushes his glasses up off his eyes and looks down directly at the dolphins. 'Who knows if they are saying anything? It's just a load of squeaks. All the stuff on the computer was probably programmed last week to make it look like they can talk. It's green propaganda. Anti-military hippy rubbish.'

I sign what the man has said to Calypso and Steve.

Calypso turns to look at the man and fires off a reply.

A news presenter looking over Rafael's shoulder reads from the screen, 'The big man with the glasses on his head and the dark shirt is right to be suspicious. How can I prove to him that I am a person like him?'

'They couldn't have programmed that yesterday,' says another reporter. 'Unless you are part of the setup.'

'Give me a break,' says the fat man with the glasses.

'So what do you say to that?' says the news presenter.

'I don't know how they are doing it, but it is a fake.'

I sign the comments for Calypso and Steve.

Steve comments and Rafael reads aloud, 'The man is an idiot. We cannot win. They will refuse to believe.'

The man with the glasses and the dark shirt waves his hand contemptuously and turns to walk away.

At which point Calypso shouts 'no.'

It isn't the first time we have heard her use her blowhole in that way but it still freaks me out. Everyone on the quayside stands transfixed.

'Listen,' she says in clearly audible English.

The news cameras roll while Calypso starts to sing the Marseillaise, the French national anthem, hesitantly at first then with growing confidence. We have never heard her sing. I wonder how on earth she had learned it then remember the years she has spent with Dad.

After ten seconds she tires and stops.

There is a burst of clicks and whistles from Steve. Rafael reads the translation aloud from the screen. 'You can choose to ignore us but that does not make us smaller, it makes you smaller. Michel told us humans were curious about everything. He was wrong.'

Clicks and whistles from Calypso.

'Yes, I know that is the French national anthem,' a news reporter reads out Calypso's words.

The cameras are flashing and we seem to have absolutely everyone's attention, even the man in the glasses and the dark shirt. Then the mood changes again. Something behind me is distracting everyone. The police vessel has approached and is now directly behind us. Standing on the prow are two armed officers and Quinton.

'I must ask everyone to leave,' the female officer calls out, rifle in hand. 'We have reason to believe that these animals may be carrying an infectious disease and pose a significant threat to local wildlife.'

I glance up and see that the news crews are still filming all the action. I drop back in the water and shout up to the crowd.

'There is nothing wrong with Calypso or Steve. They are not ill. They have no infection. This is simply an attempt to prevent the world from coming to terms with the reality that dolphins are as intelligent as we are, just different. Please help us.'

For a few seconds it seem like no-one is willing to lift a finger. Then Fred grabs Keisha's hand and pulls her toward the edge of the quay. She mumbles something about fish. Fred releases her hand, stares daggers at her, and jumps into the water. Keisha looks at me, grits her teeth and jumps in after him. There is a commotion in the crowd as someone pushes their way forwards.

'Come on,' a voice says, 'Everyone in the water. They can't shoot us all.'

A tall thin man with grey hair emerges from the crowd and leaps into the water. A woman puts her camera down by the bollard.

'I agree,' she shouts. 'Allez! Tout le monde à l'eau!'

One after another people jump in until there are at least thirty of us treading water and forming a protective ring around the dolphins. Realising there is no longer anything to read out, Rafael passes the tablet to the news presenter and throws himself in the water.

'I hope this is on the lunchtime news,' one of the swimmers shouts up at the camera crews.

'The whole thing has been streaming live across Germany since the boat docked,' the cameraman shouts back.

'And on Euronews,' shouts a presenter.

Among the handful of people still out of the water, standing among the discarded cameras and microphones, is the man who started off as the star of the show. He looks completely alone and lost. I catch his eye and wave.

'Come on, Mr Bronson. Amelia and Quinton are both wrong, you do care about this. And it has nothing to do with viewing figures, or twenty to thirty five demographics, or any of that other bull. You care because you're a decent guy and you know it matters.'

He looks down at me like I am the first person who has seen him as an ordinary human being for as long as he can remember. His face bursting into a massive grin, he runs and jumps.

I turn in the water and face the tall thin man who was the first to jump in. He is hugging Steve and Calypso like they are his best friends.

'Thanks, Dad,' I say.

78

'The reporters can wait. I want to go to the hospital. Right now.'

'No, Sam. It has taken nine years to get here; this is bigger than you or me. Or Mum. We finish this then we leave.' Dad is speaking quietly, holding my shoulders, looking me straight in the eye. 'Right?'

I nod reluctantly.

Dad returns to the table and the two waiting news crews. A few minutes ago I was on a high. Now the green dining room seems muted and remote, like standing in the dark peering into a giant fish tank; people talking about stuff that no longer matters, their facial expressions and chatter meaningless and foreign. Taking a deep breath, I rejoin the others across the room.

'Here's my star!' Wesley says as I approach. He is in his element, hands in pockets, playing to the cameras, reporters hanging on his every word. 'You news guys must stop thinking that I am the only star in the room. I mean these kids. Incredible.' Wesley points at Fred, Keisha, Rafa and me. 'Actors like me, you know, we're just playing at it, but Sam, Keisha, Fred and Ste … Rafael … got it right this time, Raffie! High five!'

Rafa makes an effort, but watching him high five is like watching the Queen juggling eggs while wobbling about on a unicycle. Uncomfortable.

Not that Wesley seems to notice. 'Anyway,' he continues, 'the stuff they've been through. That's real!' He grabs us all for a group hug while the camera flashes go off. 'This is real, man. These are my heroes. OK?' Wesley laughs his biggest laugh. 'Now y'all have to excuse me,' he says in a phony southern belle accent, 'wet eggplant purple really isn't my thing.'

Wesley removes his wet jacket and, wrinkling his nose theatrically and holding the jacket at arm's length between thumb and finger like a soiled nappy, he hands it to Quinton. 'Where's Gorspan when you need her, Quintie?'

With a subdued Quinton trailing behind him, Wesley heads for the door. 'Back in five, kids,' he calls over his shoulder. 'Then it's fate di flerrs. Party time!'

'I still can't get over your dad being here in Nice,' Rafa says, looking at Dad showing a reporter something on his laptop. 'It's fantastic. You must be so happy.'

'Yes, fantastic.' I say, struggling to keep my voice sounding light, desperate for Dad to finish his interview. How can Dad keep this up, this superhuman focusing on one thing and blocking out another?

A tug at my sleeve.

'Are we going with Wesley? Fred signs. 'To open the parade with him?'

'I need to talk with Dad.' I want to hug Fred tight and keep him close, but I don't want to alarm him.

'Is Dad coming?' It is the first time Fred has referred to Dad.

'Can you give me a minute with your sister?' Rafa asks Fred.

Keisha grabs Fred's arm and mouths the word lurve, with big rolling eyes thrown in for good measure. They wander off to stare out of the window at the festival floats gathering on the quayside. I worry about Keisha, a nine-year-old girl alone, except for us. What awaits her back in Liverpool? One of the reporters has told us that the Italian media have been covering the story of the young English girl who disappeared after a hotel explosion on Elba. He believes that the police are on their way, along with someone from the British Embassy in France. Keisha may never get to see the parade. In my mind I see her in the harbour in Bastia running across the road towards Fred and Sven. Where is Sven?

'So talk to me, Sam.'

I jump. I have forgotten that Rafa is standing next to me.

'What's wrong?'

'What do you mean?'

'Come on. I'm not stupid.'

'I need to talk with Dad, that's all.'

'That's not all. It's your mum, isn't it?'

I just stare back at him, not wanting to talk, not wanting my voice to tremble.

Rafa takes me in his arms and hugs me. My body is shaking, my head on his shoulder. I see Keisha across the room and I pull away. Too late, she has already pulled Fred round to see.

'Mum's in a coma.' I wipe my face on my sleeve. 'Dad says not to worry but I can't …' I stop, if I say any more I will cry.

'It's OK,' Rafa says softly. 'She'll be OK.'

'Excuse me.' It's one of the journalists, a woman about Mum's age. 'Are you feeling all right?'

'It's all a bit emotional,' I say vaguely.

'I can imagine.'

No, you can't imagine.

'You kids have had a tough time. Irene Dassault, Le Monde. I was wondering, do you have any evidence or proof to support your story? Any photos perhaps?'

'Can it wait?' Rafa says, trying to protect me.

'Of course, we were just …'

'It's OK,' I smile, getting back into gear.

Keisha and Fred have returned.

'Photos of the prehistoric cave with the paintings?' the reporter says, pressing on, keen to beat the rest of the media. 'The fishing nets at island, the baby dolphin, that kind of thing. Photos that confirm your story.'

I shake my head.

'Sam, yer don't know nothing, do you? She's as meff as her kid brother, that one. I filmed the whole thing on his mobile.'

Rafa and the journalist and I stare down at Keisha.

'Are you serious?' I say.

'Why wouldn't I be?' Keisha stares back up at us, arms akimbo. 'What do you think I was doing?'

I turn to Rafa. He shakes his head. 'My smart phone fell out of my pocket when I jumped in the harbour. It's under the boat somewhere.'

Easy come, easy go.

'Sorry,' I say to the reporter.

'Doesn't matter,' Keisha says. 'I uploaded it all as we went along. It's all on me blog. Scousers aren't daft, you know. Give us yer iPad and I'll show you.'

The journalist hands Keisha her tablet. Across the room, Dad's interview has finished.

'You go to the hospital with your dad, and I'll go with Wesley and the kids,' Rafa says.

I give Rafa a quick kiss on the cheek. I don't care what Keisha thinks.

'What's that for?' he asks, smiling.

Rafa's eyes are beautiful when he smiles.

'I'll see you later,' I say. 'I'll quickly check with the captain that we are OK leaving our stuff on board.'

'I can do that,' Rafa volunteers.

'Wesley has said there are some dry clothes we can wear,' Dad says behind me. 'They won't let us into the hospital like this. I'll meet you on deck in fifteen minutes.'

We both go to shower and change. I don't usually do dresses but Tim has brought a selection of Italian designer dresses, one of which, in deep blue, looks pretty cool on me.

Back out on deck I find Dad hasn't yet appeared but I spot Rafa on the lower deck, sitting at a table chatting with the captain. I walk down the steps to join them. Rafa does a double take when he sees me. A bottle sits chilling in a silver bucket. The captain is sipping from a champagne flute. He pushes a bowl of olives and nuts towards me.

'Take a seat, you look like you need a rest. Shall I ask Tim for more glasses? Hoping I would bump into you. Do you know, by any chance, who snuck off with one of our dry suits and some scuba gear? Noticed the store-room door was open.'

I take an olive, keeping an eye out for Dad.

'Now this will surprise you, Sam. Was telling Rafael here, alongside the missing gear, I found Mr Bronson's secretary, bound and gagged and with a bit of a nasty bump on her head. Volunteered to call her an ambulance but, for some unfathomable reason, she seemed rather embarrassed and said that she preferred a couple of Paracetamol and a good night's sleep. Strange, don't you think?'

'Very strange, isn't it?' I say, exchanging glances with Rafa. 'Can't help you.'

'Pity. That man who came on board with you, any idea where he's gone?'

'We've been asking ourselves the same question,' Rafa says.

'Should organise a search. In case he fell overboard. What's his name?'

'To be honest, I'm not sure we know,' I say.

The captain sighs and takes a sip of wine. Across the harbour, a bunch of youths on motorbikes are weaving back and forth between the bollards in the late afternoon sun. Where's Dad?

'Still, all told, it turned out a little more interesting than most trips.' The captain holds his wine glass up towards us. 'Cheers.'

'It beats the missing rocket in the lobster salad story,' I suggest.

'Quite so, quite so.'

'Sam.' Dad is peering over the rail on the deck above. 'Shall we go?'

I jump to my feet. 'My Mum's in hospital,' I explain.

'The captain says we can leave our stuff until …' Rafa starts, but is interrupted by a cacophony of clicks and whistles.

'Fancy introducing me to your dolphin chums, while you're still on my yacht?' The captain asks, looking down at Calypso and Steve.

'Maybe in a few days' time. If we're still your guests.'

'Cheeky.'

Christian Vassie

Moon Pool

Part One of the Moon Pool Trilogy

It's nine years since Sam Blanchard's marine biologist dad disappeared. All that remains of him is the shared love of wild animals that feeds and shields her heart.

Winning a writing competition, fifteen-year-old Sam is invited to explain to a thousand politicians why the natural world matters. Scary. But she never turns down a challenge.

As she steps from the podium she has shared with Rafael, the other competition winner, Sam is handed a scribbled note that claims her father is not dead. His life hangs by a thread. Before it is too late he wants to see her and share a secret.

A secret that will change the course of history.

Sam and Rafael race across Europe to find Sam's dad. How long do they have? Why does Sam feel everyone is hiding things from her? And does Rafael ever not wear a tie?

An epic tale of discovery, betrayal and adventure. The stakes are higher than Sam could possibly have imagined.

Christian Vassie

Who the waves wake

Part Three of the Moon Pool Trilogy

Staring at the coffin, sixteen-year-old Sam Blanchard hopes that what is left of her family will be left in peace. Some hope. Her dad, Michel, rushes from the funeral to a marine institute where the dolphins are undergoing tests to prove their sentience.

The enigmatic Sven arrives with suspiciously impeccable timing. Michel has disappeared and the institute reports the dolphins dead. Sam is one of only three people in the world able to make sense of what has happened.

With Rafael persuaded to join Sam's quest for answers, the trail leads to an old adversary, a shipping company in Rotterdam, an ancient treasure and the hardest choices Sam will ever have to make.

"An action packed and thought-provoking rollercoaster you cannot put down."

"The explosive heart-wrenching conclusion to the Moon Pool Trilogy stayed with me for days."

"I feared turning the pages but could not stop turning them."